# Unlocking Your Best Self: A Guide to Building Mental Wellness

**Mental Health: A Guide to Improvement**

# Unlocking Your Best Self: A Guide to Building Mental Wellness

## Mental Health: A Guide to Improvement

Lucien Gahiel

*Copyright*

**Unlocking Your Best Self: A Guide to Building Mental Wellness
Mental Health: A Guide to Improvement**

*Author:* Lucien Gahiel

**Copyright © 2024 by Lucien Gahiel
All Rights Reserved**

No part of this publication may be reproduced, distributed, or transmitted in any form or by any means, including photocopying, recording, or other electronic or mechanical methods, without the prior written permission of the publisher, except in the case of brief quotations embodied in critical reviews and certain other noncommercial uses permitted by copyright law.

**Published by:** Amazon

**Disclaimer:** The information provided in this book is intended for general informational purposes only and should not be considered as professional advice. Consult with a qualified mental health professional for specific guidance related to your situation.

**For more information, please visit:** Amazon

**Printed Amazon
First Edition**

# Dedication

To all those who have faced the shadows and still strive towards the light,

To my family and friends, whose unwavering support and love have been my anchor in times of turbulence,

To the mental health professionals and advocates who tirelessly work to bring hope and healing to others,

And to every individual on their journey towards better mental wellness, may you find strength, courage, and the joy of discovering your best self.

This book is dedicated to you.

**Lucien Gahiel**

**Table of Contents**

**Part 1: Understanding Mental Health**

- Chapter 1: What is Mental Health?
- Defining mental health
- common conditions,
- importance of seeking help

## Defining Mental Health

**Mental health** encompasses emotional, psychological, and social well-being. It influences how individuals think, feel, and behave, affecting their ability to handle stress, relate to others, and make decisions. Mental health is an integral part of overall health and well-being.

## Common Mental Health Conditions

1. **Anxiety Disorders:** Characterized by excessive fear or worry. Common types include generalized anxiety disorder (GAD), panic disorder, and social anxiety disorder.

2. **Mood Disorders:** These involve disturbances in mood. The most common mood disorders are depression and bipolar disorder.
3. **Psychotic Disorders:** These involve distorted thinking and awareness. Schizophrenia is a prominent example, marked by hallucinations and delusions.
4. **Eating Disorders:** Involve extreme emotions, attitudes, and behaviors surrounding weight and food. Examples include anorexia nervosa, bulimia nervosa, and binge-eating disorder.
5. **Personality Disorders:** These involve enduring patterns of behavior, cognition, and inner experience, deviating from cultural expectations. Borderline personality disorder and antisocial personality disorder are examples.
6. **Obsessive-Compulsive and Related Disorders:** Characterized by obsessive thoughts and compulsive actions. Obsessive-compulsive disorder (OCD) and body dysmorphic disorder are included in this category.
7. **Post-Traumatic Stress Disorder (PTSD):** Develops after exposure to a traumatic event, resulting in severe anxiety, flashbacks, and changes in mood and behavior.

## Importance of Seeking Help

- **Early Intervention:** Seeking help early can prevent conditions from worsening and improve long-term outcomes.
- **Improved Quality of Life:** Treatment can help individuals manage symptoms, leading to a better quality of life.
- **Support and Resources:** Access to professional support provides coping strategies and resources for managing mental health.
- **Reduction of Stigma:** Seeking help can reduce the stigma associated with mental health issues, encouraging others to do the same.
- **Preventive Care:** Addressing mental health proactively can prevent the development of more severe conditions and improve overall health.

## Conclusion

Mental health is a crucial aspect of overall well-being, affecting how individuals think, feel, and act. Understanding common mental health conditions and the importance of seeking help can lead to better management and improved quality of life. It is essential to address mental health issues with the same seriousness as physical health, ensuring access to the necessary support and resources.

- **Chapter 2: The Spectrum of Mental Health**
- Normalcy vs. needing help
- destigmatization

## The Spectrum of Mental Health

Mental health exists on a spectrum, ranging from well-being and resilience to varying degrees of distress and dysfunction. This spectrum acknowledges that everyone experiences fluctuations in their mental health based on life events, stressors, and personal circumstances.

### Normalcy vs. Needing Help

**Normalcy:**

- **Resilience:** Individuals can handle stress and recover from setbacks.
- **Positive Well-being:** Feelings of contentment, happiness, and satisfaction with life.
- **Effective Functioning:** The ability to maintain relationships, perform at work or school, and engage in daily activities.
- **Transient Symptoms:** Occasional feelings of sadness, anxiety, or stress that do not persist or significantly interfere with life.

**Needing Help:**

- **Persistent Symptoms:** Ongoing feelings of sadness, anxiety, or stress that last for weeks or longer.
- **Interference with Daily Life:** Difficulty performing everyday tasks, maintaining relationships, or functioning at work or school.
- **Physical Symptoms:** Changes in sleep, appetite, energy levels, and physical health due to emotional distress.
- **Negative Thought Patterns:** Persistent negative thinking, hopelessness, or thoughts of self-harm or suicide.

## Destigmatization of Mental Health

**Understanding and Awareness:**

- **Education:** Promoting awareness and understanding of mental health conditions to dispel myths and misconceptions.
- **Media Representation:** Positive and accurate portrayals of mental health in media to normalize conversations and reduce fear.

**Encouraging Open Dialogue:**

- **Safe Spaces:** Creating environments where individuals feel safe to share their experiences without judgment.
- **Support Networks:** Building strong support networks among family, friends, and communities to provide emotional and practical support.

**Access to Resources:**

- **Healthcare Services:** Ensuring access to mental health services, including therapy, counseling, and medication.
- **Workplace Support:** Implementing mental health policies and programs in workplaces to support employees.

**Role of Advocacy:**

- **Public Campaigns:** Advocacy groups can run campaigns to raise awareness and encourage positive attitudes toward mental health.
- **Policy Change:** Advocating for policies that support mental health care and protect the rights of individuals with mental health conditions.

## Conclusion

Mental health exists on a spectrum, and everyone can experience fluctuations between well-being and distress. Recognizing when help is needed and seeking it without shame is crucial for maintaining mental health. Destigmatizing mental health through education, open dialogue, access to resources, and advocacy can lead to a more understanding and supportive society, encouraging individuals to seek help when needed and fostering overall well-being.

- **Chapter 3: Recognizing Signs & Symptoms**
- **Common signs of anxiety**
- **depression**
- **stress,**

## Recognizing Signs & Symptoms

Understanding the common signs and symptoms of mental health conditions such as anxiety, depression, and stress is crucial for early intervention and effective management. Here is a guide to recognizing these conditions:

### Anxiety

**Common Signs:**

- **Persistent Worry:** Excessive fear or worry about various aspects of life (work, social situations, health).
- **Restlessness:** Feeling on edge, restless, or tense.
- **Physical Symptoms:** Increased heart rate, sweating, trembling, shortness of breath, gastrointestinal issues.
- **Irritability:** Easily annoyed or angered.
- **Sleep Disturbances:** Difficulty falling asleep, staying asleep, or experiencing restful sleep.
- **Concentration Issues:** Trouble focusing or finding one's mind going blank.

### Depression

**Common Signs:**

- **Persistent Sadness:** Ongoing feelings of sadness, emptiness, or hopelessness.
- **Loss of Interest:** Diminished interest or pleasure in almost all activities, including hobbies and social interactions.
- **Appetite Changes:** Significant weight loss or gain, or changes in appetite.
- **Sleep Problems:** Insomnia or excessive sleeping.
- **Fatigue:** Loss of energy and increased fatigue.
- **Feelings of Worthlessness:** Excessive or inappropriate guilt, feelings of worthlessness or helplessness.
- **Cognitive Issues:** Difficulty thinking, concentrating, or making decisions.
- **Physical Symptoms:** Aches, pains, or digestive problems without a clear physical cause.
- **Suicidal Thoughts:** Thoughts of death or suicide, or attempts at self-harm.

### Stress

**Common Signs:**

- **Emotional Distress:** Feelings of being overwhelmed, anxious, or irritable.

- **Cognitive Symptoms:** Trouble concentrating, memory problems, negative thinking patterns.
- **Behavioral Changes:** Changes in behavior, such as withdrawing from social activities, procrastination, or increased use of alcohol/drugs.
- **Physical Symptoms:** Headaches, muscle tension, fatigue, stomach issues, sleep disturbances.
- **Mood Swings:** Rapid changes in mood, including frustration and anger.
- **Decreased Productivity:** Drop in performance at work or school.

## Recognizing Other Mental Health Conditions

### Obsessive-Compulsive Disorder (OCD):

- **Obsessions:** Recurrent, persistent, unwanted thoughts or urges.
- **Compulsions:** Repetitive behaviors or mental acts performed to reduce anxiety related to obsessions.

### Bipolar Disorder:

- **Manic Episodes:** Periods of abnormally elevated mood, energy, and activity levels, often accompanied by reckless behavior.
- **Depressive Episodes:** Periods of low mood, similar to depression.

### Post-Traumatic Stress Disorder (PTSD):

- **Re-experiencing:** Flashbacks, nightmares, or intrusive thoughts about a traumatic event.
- **Avoidance:** Avoiding reminders of the trauma, including places, people, and activities.
- **Hyperarousal:** Being easily startled, feeling tense, or having difficulty sleeping.

## Conclusion

Recognizing the signs and symptoms of mental health conditions such as anxiety, depression, and stress is essential for early intervention and support. Being aware of these signs can help individuals seek appropriate help and resources, improving their overall well-being and quality of life. Encouraging open conversations about mental health and providing support can make a significant difference in the lives of those affected.

- **Chapter 4: The Impact of Mental Health**
- **Physical health**
- **relationships**
- **work performance**

## The Impact of Mental Health

Mental health significantly influences various aspects of an individual's life, including physical health, relationships, and work performance. Understanding these impacts can help highlight the importance of maintaining good mental health and seeking help when needed.

### Physical Health

### Chronic Illnesses:

- Mental health conditions like depression and anxiety can exacerbate chronic illnesses such as heart disease, diabetes, and arthritis.
- Stress and anxiety can lead to elevated blood pressure and increased risk of cardiovascular problems.

### Immune System:

- Poor mental health can weaken the immune system, making individuals more susceptible to infections and illnesses.
- Chronic stress can result in prolonged inflammatory responses, negatively affecting overall health.

### Sleep and Appetite:

- Mental health issues often disrupt sleep patterns, leading to insomnia or hypersomnia, which can further exacerbate mental and physical health problems.
- Changes in appetite, whether increased or decreased, can lead to significant weight loss or gain, impacting nutritional health.

**Relationships**

**Communication:**

- Mental health conditions can impair an individual's ability to communicate effectively, leading to misunderstandings and conflicts.
- Anxiety and depression can cause withdrawal from social interactions, reducing the quality and quantity of relationships.

**Emotional Intimacy:**

- Difficulty in managing emotions can hinder emotional intimacy and trust in relationships.
- Partners or family members may feel helpless or frustrated if they do not understand the individual's mental health challenges.

**Social Isolation:**

- Mental health issues can lead to social withdrawal, increasing feelings of loneliness and isolation.
- Social isolation can, in turn, worsen mental health conditions, creating a vicious cycle.

**Work Performance**

**Productivity:**

- Mental health problems can significantly reduce concentration, decision-making ability, and overall productivity.
- Increased absenteeism due to mental health issues can affect job performance and career progression.

**Workplace Relationships:**

- Stress and mood disorders can strain relationships with colleagues and supervisors, leading to a tense and uncooperative work environment.
- Poor mental health can result in decreased collaboration and teamwork.

**Job Satisfaction:**

- Individuals with mental health conditions may experience lower job satisfaction and motivation.
- A lack of job satisfaction can lead to higher turnover rates and reduced organizational commitment.

## Conclusion

Mental health has a profound impact on physical health, relationships, and work performance. Recognizing these effects underscores the importance of addressing mental health issues promptly and comprehensively. Ensuring access to mental health resources, promoting a supportive environment, and fostering open dialogue about mental health can help mitigate these impacts, leading to healthier, more productive lives.

Part 2: Building a Foundation for Wellbeing

### Chapter 5: Self-Care Essentials

**Sleep,**

**nutrition,**

**Exercise,**

**mindfulness**

## Self-Care Essentials

Maintaining good mental health requires a comprehensive approach, incorporating various self-care practices. Key components of self-care include sleep, nutrition, exercise, and mindfulness. These practices can significantly enhance overall well-being and help manage stress and mental health conditions.

### Sleep

**Importance:**

- Sleep is essential for cognitive function, emotional regulation, and physical health.
- Quality sleep supports memory consolidation, mood stability, and overall mental resilience.

**Tips for Better Sleep:**

- **Consistent Schedule:** Go to bed and wake up at the same time every day, even on weekends.
- **Sleep Environment:** Create a quiet, dark, and cool sleeping environment. Use blackout curtains, earplugs, or white noise machines if needed.
- **Limit Screen Time:** Avoid screens (phones, computers, TVs) at least an hour before bed to reduce blue light exposure that can interfere with sleep.
- **Relaxation Techniques:** Practice relaxation techniques such as deep breathing, progressive muscle relaxation, or reading a book before bed.

### Nutrition

**Importance:**

- Proper nutrition fuels the body and mind, providing essential nutrients for brain function and mood regulation.
- A balanced diet can improve energy levels, concentration, and overall mental health.

**Tips for Healthy Eating:**

- **Balanced Diet:** Include a variety of fruits, vegetables, whole grains, lean proteins, and healthy fats in your diet.
- **Regular Meals:** Eat regular meals and healthy snacks to maintain blood sugar levels and avoid energy crashes.
- **Hydration:** Drink plenty of water throughout the day to stay hydrated and support bodily functions.
- **Limit Processed Foods:** Reduce intake of processed foods, sugary snacks, and excessive caffeine and alcohol.

### Exercise

**Importance:**

- Regular physical activity improves mood, reduces anxiety and depression symptoms, and enhances cognitive function.
- Exercise releases endorphins, which are natural mood lifters.

**Tips for Staying Active:**

- **Find Enjoyable Activities:** Choose physical activities you enjoy, such as walking, cycling, dancing, or swimming.

- **Consistency:** Aim for at least 150 minutes of moderate-intensity exercise or 75 minutes of vigorous-intensity exercise per week.
- **Incorporate Movement:** Integrate physical activity into your daily routine, such as taking the stairs, walking during breaks, or stretching.
- **Social Exercise:** Join group classes or exercise with friends to stay motivated and make physical activity more enjoyable.

**Mindfulness**

**Importance:**

- Mindfulness practices help reduce stress, improve focus, and enhance emotional regulation.
- Being present in the moment can increase awareness and acceptance of thoughts and feelings.

**Tips for Practicing Mindfulness:**

- **Meditation:** Practice mindfulness meditation by focusing on your breath and observing your thoughts without judgment.
- **Mindful Breathing:** Take deep, slow breaths and focus on the sensation of breathing to calm the mind and body.
- **Mindful Activities:** Engage in activities like yoga, tai chi, or mindful walking, which combine physical movement with mindfulness.
- **Daily Mindfulness:** Incorporate mindfulness into daily activities, such as eating, cleaning, or commuting, by paying full attention to the experience.

## Conclusion

Self-care is essential for maintaining mental health and overall well-being. Prioritizing sleep, nutrition, exercise, and mindfulness can help manage stress, improve mood, and enhance cognitive function. By incorporating these self-care practices into daily life, individuals can build resilience and support their mental health effectively.

### Chapter 6: Building Healthy Relationships

Communication skills,

support systems,

setting boundaries

# Building Healthy Relationships

Healthy relationships are crucial for mental well-being and overall quality of life. They provide support, companionship, and a sense of belonging. Building and maintaining healthy relationships involves effective communication skills, strong support systems, and the ability to set boundaries.

### Communication Skills

**Importance:**

- Effective communication is the foundation of any healthy relationship.
- Clear and respectful communication fosters understanding, reduces conflicts, and strengthens connections.

**Tips for Effective Communication:**

- **Active Listening:** Listen attentively without interrupting. Show that you understand by nodding, maintaining eye contact, and providing feedback.
- **Expressing Feelings:** Use "I" statements to express your feelings and needs without blaming or criticizing. For example, "I feel upset when you don't call me back."
- **Nonverbal Communication:** Be aware of your body language, facial expressions, and tone of voice. These can convey as much, if not more, than words.
- **Clarification:** Ask questions if something is unclear to ensure you fully understand the other person's perspective.
- **Conflict Resolution:** Address conflicts calmly and respectfully. Focus on finding solutions rather than assigning blame.

### Support Systems

**Importance:**

- Having a robust support system provides emotional, informational, and practical support during challenging times.
- Support systems can include family, friends, colleagues, and support groups.

- **Tips for Building Support Systems:**

- **Quality Over Quantity:** Focus on building a few strong, meaningful relationships rather than numerous superficial ones.
- **Reach Out:** Don't hesitate to ask for help or support when needed. Sharing your struggles can strengthen your connections.
- **Be Supportive:** Offer support to others. Being there for someone else can also strengthen your own support network.
- **Join Groups:** Participate in community groups, clubs, or online communities that align with your interests and values.
- **Professional Help:** Sometimes, seeking support from a mental health professional can be beneficial.

**Setting Boundaries**

**Importance:**

- Setting boundaries is essential for maintaining healthy relationships and protecting your mental and emotional well-being.
- Boundaries help define what is acceptable and what is not, ensuring mutual respect.

**Tips for Setting Boundaries:**

- **Know Your Limits:** Understand your own limits and what you are comfortable with in relationships.
- **Be Clear and Direct:** Communicate your boundaries clearly and assertively. For example, "I need some alone time after work to unwind."
- **Consistency:** Enforce your boundaries consistently. It's important to follow through on what you have communicated.
- **Respect Others' Boundaries:** Just as you set boundaries, respect the boundaries set by others.
- **Adjust as Needed:** Boundaries can change over time. Reassess and adjust them as necessary to suit your current needs and circumstances.

## Conclusion

Building healthy relationships is integral to mental and emotional well-being. By honing communication skills, cultivating strong support systems, and setting and respecting boundaries, individuals can foster relationships that are supportive, respectful, and fulfilling. These practices help create a balanced and harmonious social environment, contributing to overall life satisfaction and mental health.

**Chapter 7: Stress Management Techniques**

**Relaxation methods,**

 **time management,**

 **coping skills**

# Stress Management Techniques

Effectively managing stress is essential for maintaining mental and physical health. Various techniques can help reduce stress and enhance overall well-being, including relaxation methods, time management strategies, and coping skills.

### Relaxation Methods

### Importance:

- Relaxation techniques help calm the mind and body, reducing the physiological effects of stress.
- Regular practice of relaxation methods can improve mood, increase focus, and promote overall health.

### Common Relaxation Techniques:

- **Deep Breathing:** Focus on taking slow, deep breaths. Inhale deeply through the nose, hold for a few seconds, and exhale slowly through the mouth. This helps activate the body's relaxation response.
- **Progressive Muscle Relaxation (PMR):** Gradually tense and then relax each muscle group in the body, starting from the toes and working up to the head. This technique can help release physical tension.
- **Meditation:** Practice mindfulness or guided meditation to focus the mind and reduce stress. Apps and online resources can provide guided sessions for beginners.
- **Visualization:** Imagine a peaceful scene or place. Use all your senses to make the visualization as vivid as possible, helping to create a sense of calm and relaxation.
- **Yoga and Tai Chi:** These practices combine physical movement, breathing exercises, and meditation to promote relaxation and reduce stress.

### Time Management

**Importance:**

- Effective time management can help reduce stress by improving productivity and reducing feelings of being overwhelmed.
- Prioritizing tasks and managing time efficiently can lead to a more balanced and fulfilling life.

**Tips for Better Time Management:**

- **Prioritize Tasks:** Identify the most important tasks and focus on completing them first. Use tools like the Eisenhower Matrix to categorize tasks by urgency and importance.
- **Set Realistic Goals:** Break larger tasks into smaller, manageable steps and set achievable goals. This can prevent procrastination and reduce stress.
- **Create a Schedule:** Use planners, calendars, or digital tools to plan your day, week, or month. Allocate specific times for tasks, breaks, and leisure activities.
- **Avoid Multitasking:** Focus on one task at a time to increase efficiency and reduce errors. Multitasking can lead to increased stress and decreased productivity.
- **Delegate Tasks:** If possible, delegate tasks to others to lighten your workload. This can help free up time for more critical tasks or self-care.

## Coping Skills

**Importance:**

- Developing effective coping skills can help manage stress in a healthy way, reducing its impact on your life.
- Coping skills can improve resilience, making it easier to handle future stressors.

**Common Coping Skills:**

- **Problem-Solving:** Identify the source of stress and develop a plan to address it. Break the problem into smaller parts and tackle each part step by step.

- **Cognitive Restructuring:** Challenge and change negative thought patterns. Replace irrational or negative thoughts with more realistic and positive ones.
- **Social Support:** Reach out to friends, family, or support groups for emotional support. Talking about your stress can provide relief and new perspectives.
- **Healthy Lifestyle:** Maintain a balanced diet, exercise regularly, and get enough sleep. A healthy lifestyle can improve your ability to cope with stress.
- **Hobbies and Interests:** Engage in activities that you enjoy and that relax you. This can provide a break from stress and help you recharge.
- **Mindfulness Practices:** Incorporate mindfulness into your daily routine. This can include mindful eating, walking, or simply paying attention to your surroundings and sensations in the present moment.

## Conclusion

Managing stress effectively involves a combination of relaxation methods, time management strategies, and coping skills. Incorporating these techniques into daily life can help reduce stress, improve overall well-being, and enhance the ability to handle life's challenges. By taking proactive steps to manage stress, individuals can lead healthier, more balanced lives.

### Chapter 8: The Power of a Positive Mindset

Thought patterns,

Gratitude,

Reframing negativity

## The Power of a Positive Mindset

A positive mindset can significantly impact overall well-being, enhancing mental health, emotional resilience, and life satisfaction. Adopting positive thought patterns, practicing gratitude, and reframing negativity are effective ways to cultivate a positive mindset.

**Thought Patterns**

**Importance:**

- Positive thought patterns can improve emotional health, increase motivation, and foster a sense of well-being.
- Negative thought patterns can lead to increased stress, anxiety, and depression.

**Developing Positive Thought Patterns:**

- **Self-Awareness:** Recognize and monitor your thoughts. Pay attention to recurring negative thoughts and how they affect your mood and behavior.
- **Positive Affirmations:** Use positive affirmations to challenge and replace negative thoughts. For example, replace "I can't do this" with "I am capable and will do my best."
- **Focus on Strengths:** Concentrate on your strengths and achievements rather than dwelling on weaknesses or failures. Acknowledge your progress and efforts.
- **Surround Yourself with Positivity:** Engage with positive influences, such as supportive friends, inspiring books, or motivational content. Limit exposure to negative media and people.

**Gratitude**

**Importance:**

- Practicing gratitude can enhance mood, reduce stress, and improve overall life satisfaction.
- Gratitude shifts focus from what is lacking to what is abundant, fostering a sense of appreciation and contentment.

**Practicing Gratitude:**

- **Gratitude Journaling:** Write down things you are grateful for daily or weekly. Reflecting on these entries can boost your mood and provide perspective during challenging times.
- **Expressing Thanks:** Regularly express gratitude to others. Thank people for their kindness, support, or positive influence in your life.

- **Gratitude Meditation:** Incorporate gratitude into meditation by focusing on things you are thankful for. This practice can deepen your sense of appreciation.
- **Gratitude Rituals:** Create daily or weekly rituals that remind you to be grateful, such as sharing positive experiences with a loved one or reflecting on the day's blessings before bed.

### Reframing Negativity

**Importance:**

- Reframing negativity involves changing the way you perceive and respond to negative situations, helping to reduce their impact on your mental health.
- This practice can enhance problem-solving skills, increase resilience, and promote a more balanced perspective.

**Techniques for Reframing Negativity:**

- **Cognitive Restructuring:** Challenge negative thoughts by questioning their validity and considering alternative, more positive perspectives. For example, instead of thinking "I'll never get through this," consider "This is challenging, but I can find a way to manage it."
- **Finding the Silver Lining:** Look for positive aspects or lessons in negative situations. For example, a difficult project at work might be stressful, but it can also be an opportunity to develop new skills.
- **Acceptance and Commitment:** Accept that negative thoughts and emotions are a natural part of life. Focus on what you can control and commit to actions that align with your values and goals.
- **Perspective Taking:** Consider how you might view the situation from a different perspective or how someone else might perceive it. This can help you see the situation in a new light and reduce negative bias.

## Conclusion

Cultivating a positive mindset through positive thought patterns, gratitude, and reframing negativity can significantly enhance mental and emotional well-being. These practices help build resilience, improve mood, and foster a more fulfilling and balanced life. By consciously adopting a positive mindset, individuals can navigate life's challenges more effectively and enjoy greater overall satisfaction.

**Chapter 9: Building Resilience**

**Finding meaning,**

 **coping with setbacks,**

 **developing emotional intelligence**

## Building Resilience

Resilience is the ability to adapt and recover from adversity, setbacks, and stress. It involves finding meaning in challenging situations, coping effectively with setbacks, and developing emotional intelligence. Building resilience can enhance overall well-being and help individuals thrive in the face of difficulties.

### Finding Meaning

**Importance:**

- Finding meaning in life's challenges can provide a sense of purpose and motivation.
- Meaningful experiences can foster personal growth and a deeper understanding of oneself and the world.

**Strategies for Finding Meaning:**

- **Reflect on Values:** Identify your core values and consider how challenging experiences align with or impact these values. Reflecting on your values can provide direction and purpose.
- **Set Goals:** Establish short-term and long-term goals that are meaningful to you. Working towards these goals can provide a sense of accomplishment and direction.
- **Help Others:** Engaging in acts of kindness and helping others can create a sense of purpose and connection. Volunteering or supporting loved ones can be fulfilling.
- **Seek Inspiration:** Read books, watch films, or listen to stories of individuals who have found meaning in adversity. These narratives can provide perspective and motivation.

### Coping with Setbacks

**Importance:**

- Effective coping strategies can mitigate the impact of setbacks and facilitate recovery.
- Coping skills help manage stress and prevent setbacks from undermining overall well-being.

**Coping Strategies:**

- **Positive Reframing:** Reframe setbacks as opportunities for learning and growth. Focus on what you can learn from the experience and how it can contribute to your development.
- **Problem-Solving:** Break down the problem into manageable parts and develop a plan to address each part. Taking actionable steps can reduce feelings of helplessness.
- **Emotional Expression:** Allow yourself to express your emotions, whether through talking with someone you trust, journaling, or creative outlets like art or music.
- **Self-Compassion:** Practice self-compassion by treating yourself with kindness and understanding during difficult times. Acknowledge that setbacks are a normal part of life and not a reflection of your worth.
- **Mindfulness Practices:** Engage in mindfulness practices such as meditation, deep breathing, or yoga to stay grounded and reduce stress.

### Developing Emotional Intelligence

**Importance:**

- Emotional intelligence (EI) involves recognizing, understanding, and managing one's own emotions and the emotions of others.
- High EI can improve relationships, enhance communication, and foster resilience in the face of adversity.

**Components of Emotional Intelligence:**

- **Self-Awareness:** Recognize and understand your own emotions. Reflect on how your emotions influence your thoughts and behavior.
- **Self-Regulation:** Manage your emotions in healthy ways. Practice techniques like deep breathing, mindfulness, or taking a break when feeling overwhelmed.
- **Motivation:** Cultivate intrinsic motivation by setting meaningful goals and finding personal reasons to pursue them. Stay focused and resilient in the face of challenges.
- **Empathy:** Develop the ability to understand and share the feelings of others. Practice active listening and consider other people's perspectives.

- **Social Skills:** Enhance your ability to communicate effectively, resolve conflicts, and build strong relationships. Practice assertiveness and active listening in your interactions.

## Conclusion

Building resilience involves finding meaning in life's challenges, developing effective coping strategies, and enhancing emotional intelligence. These components can help individuals navigate adversity, recover from setbacks, and maintain overall well-being. By fostering resilience, individuals can not only survive difficult times but also grow and thrive in the face of them.

**Part 3: Seeking Professional Help When Needed**

- **Chapter 10: Finding the Right Therapist**
- **Types of therapy**
- **finding a good fit**
- **insurance considerations**

## Finding the Right Therapist

Choosing the right therapist is crucial for effective mental health treatment. It involves understanding different types of therapy, finding a therapist who is a good fit, and considering insurance and financial factors. Here's a guide to help you navigate this process:

**Types of Therapy**

**Cognitive Behavioral Therapy (CBT):**

- **Focus:** Identifying and changing negative thought patterns and behaviors.
- **Best For:** Depression, anxiety, phobias, PTSD, eating disorders.

**Psychodynamic Therapy:**

- **Focus:** Uncovering unconscious patterns and exploring past experiences that influence current behavior.
- **Best For:** Depression, anxiety, relationship issues, personality disorders.

**Humanistic Therapy:**

- **Focus:** Promoting personal growth and self-actualization through a non-judgmental, empathetic approach.
- **Best For:** Self-esteem issues, personal growth, existential crises.

**Dialectical Behavior Therapy (DBT):**

- **Focus:** Combining CBT with mindfulness techniques to manage emotions and reduce self-destructive behaviors.
- **Best For:** Borderline personality disorder, self-harm, chronic suicidal thoughts, eating disorders.

**Family Therapy:**

- **Focus:** Addressing family dynamics and improving communication and relationships within the family unit.
- **Best For:** Family conflicts, communication issues, dealing with major life changes, and family-based problems.

**Group Therapy:**

- **Focus:** Providing support and feedback in a group setting, often facilitated by one or more therapists.
- **Best For:** Social anxiety, addiction, support groups for specific issues like grief or chronic illness.

**Couples Therapy:**

- **Focus:** Improving communication, resolving conflicts, and enhancing intimacy between partners.
- **Best For:** Relationship issues, communication problems, premarital counseling, infidelity.

### Finding a Good Fit

**Assess Your Needs:**

- Determine what specific issues you want to address (e.g., anxiety, relationship issues).
- Consider what type of therapy might be most effective for your needs.

**Research and Referrals:**

- Ask for referrals from your primary care doctor, friends, or family.
- Use online directories (e.g., Psychology Today, TherapyDen) to find therapists in your area.

**Credentials and Specializations:**

- Ensure the therapst is licensed and certified in your state.
- Look for therapists who specialize in the issues you want to address.

**Initial Consultation:**

- Schedule a consultation to discuss your goals and see if you feel comfortable with the therapist.
- Ask about their approach to therapy, experience with your issues, and what a typical session looks like.

**Evaluate Comfort and Rapport:**

- Consider if you feel heard, understood, and respected by the therapist.
- Trust your instincts about whether the therapist is a good fit for you.

### Insurance Considerations

**Check Coverage:**

- Review your insurance policy to understand what mental health services are covered.
- Check if you need a referral from your primary care doctor to see a therapist.

**In-Network vs. Out-of-Network:**

- Find out if the therapist is in-network with your insurance plan, which can reduce out-of-pocket costs.
- If out-of-network, understand what reimbursement rates or additional costs may apply.

**Verify Costs:**

- Ask about session fees, sliding scale options, and any additional costs.
- Understand how many sessions are covered by your insurance and if there are any limits on coverage.

**Use Employer Resources:**

- Explore Employee Assistance Programs (EAPs) offered by your employer, which may provide free or low-cost counseling services.

## Conclusion

Finding the right therapist involves understanding the types of therapy available, ensuring a good fit through research and initial consultations, and considering insurance and financial aspects. Taking the time to find a therapist who meets your needs and makes you feel comfortable can significantly enhance the effectiveness of your mental health treatment and overall well-being.

Tips for improving emotional intelligence?

Improving emotional intelligence (EI) can greatly enhance personal and professional relationships, boost self-awareness, and improve overall well-being. Emotional intelligence involves understanding, managing, and effectively using emotions in yourself and others. Here are some practical tips for enhancing your emotional intelligence:

## 1. Develop Self-Awareness

- **Reflect Regularly:** Take time to reflect on your emotions and reactions. Keep a journal to note how you feel in various situations and what triggers these emotions.
- **Identify Patterns:** Look for patterns in your emotional responses. Understanding when and why you react in certain ways can help you anticipate and manage your emotions better.
- **Seek Feedback:** Ask trusted friends, family, or colleagues for feedback on your emotional reactions and interactions. Use their insights to improve your self-awareness.

## 2. Enhance Self-Regulation

- **Practice Mindfulness:** Engage in mindfulness practices such as meditation, deep breathing, or yoga to stay grounded and manage stress.
- **Develop Coping Strategies:** Identify healthy coping mechanisms for managing strong emotions, such as exercise, creative activities, or talking with a friend.
- **Pause Before Reacting:** When faced with a strong emotional reaction, take a moment to pause and reflect before responding. This can help you respond more thoughtfully rather than react impulsively.

## 3. Improve Motivation

- **Set Personal Goals:** Establish meaningful and achievable goals that align with your values and interests. This helps maintain motivation and focus.
- **Celebrate Achievements:** Acknowledge and celebrate your accomplishments, no matter how small. This reinforces positive behavior and motivation.
- **Maintain a Positive Outlook:** Focus on positive aspects of your life and practice gratitude. This can boost your overall motivation and resilience.

## 4. Enhance Empathy

- **Active Listening:** Practice active listening by fully concentrating on the speaker, reflecting on what is said, and responding thoughtfully. Avoid interrupting or making assumptions.
- **Ask Open-Ended Questions:** Encourage others to express their feelings and perspectives by asking open-ended questions. This shows genuine interest and helps you understand their viewpoints.
- **Put Yourself in Others' Shoes:** Try to see situations from others' perspectives. This can help you understand their emotions and reactions better.

## 5. Develop Social Skills

- **Improve Communication:** Work on clear and effective communication. Use "I" statements to express your feelings and needs without blaming or criticizing others.
- **Resolve Conflicts Constructively:** Approach conflicts with a problem-solving mindset. Focus on finding solutions rather than assigning blame.
- **Build Relationships:** Invest time in building and maintaining strong relationships. Show appreciation, offer support, and be reliable in your interactions.

## 6. Practice Emotional Regulation

- **Recognize Triggers:** Identify situations or people that trigger strong emotional responses and develop strategies to manage these triggers effectively.
- **Use Relaxation Techniques:** Incorporate relaxation techniques such as deep breathing, progressive muscle relaxation, or visualization to manage stress and regulate emotions.
- **Seek Support When Needed:** Don't hesitate to seek support from a mental health professional if you struggle with managing emotions or dealing with emotional challenges.

## 7. Cultivate Emotional Resilience

- **Embrace Challenges:** View challenges as opportunities for growth and learning. Approach difficulties with a resilient mindset.
- **Learn from Experiences:** Reflect on past experiences and how you handled them. Use these insights to improve your emotional responses in future situations.
- **Develop Problem-Solving Skills:** Strengthen your ability to solve problems effectively, which can help you manage stress and emotional challenges more effectively.

## Conclusion

Improving emotional intelligence involves enhancing self-awareness, self-regulation, motivation, empathy, and social skills. By practicing these tips and integrating them into your daily life, you can foster better relationships, manage emotions more effectively, and enhance your overall emotional well-being. Developing emotional intelligence is an ongoing process that contributes to personal growth and more fulfilling interactions with others.

### How can I practice mindfulness daily?

Practicing mindfulness daily can significantly enhance your mental well-being, reduce stress, and improve overall quality of life. Mindfulness involves focusing on the present moment with an attitude of acceptance and non-judgment. Here are practical ways to incorporate mindfulness into your daily routine:

### 1. Start with Mindful Breathing

- **Daily Practice:** Spend 5-10 minutes each day focusing on your breath. Sit comfortably, close your eyes, and pay attention to the sensation of your breath as it enters and leaves your body. If your mind wanders, gently bring your focus back to your breath.
- **Breathing Exercises:** Practice different breathing techniques, such as deep diaphragmatic breathing, box breathing (inhale for 4 counts, hold for 4 counts, exhale for 4 counts, hold for 4 counts), or 4-7-8 breathing (inhale for 4 counts, hold for 7 counts, exhale for 8 counts).

### 2. Incorporate Mindfulness into Daily Activities

- **Mindful Eating:** Pay full attention to the taste, texture, and aroma of your food. Eat slowly, savor each bite, and notice how the food makes you feel.
- **Mindful Walking:** During walks, focus on the sensation of your feet touching the ground, the rhythm of your steps, and the environment around you. Observe the sights, sounds, and smells without judgment.
- **Mindful Listening:** Practice active listening in conversations by fully focusing on the speaker, avoiding interruptions, and acknowledging their emotions and perspectives.

### 3. Use Mindfulness Apps and Resources

- **Meditation Apps:** Utilize apps like Headspace, Calm, Insight Timer, or 10% Happier for guided mindfulness and meditation sessions. These apps offer various practices and tools for incorporating mindfulness into your routine.
- **Online Resources:** Explore mindfulness websites and YouTube channels that provide guided meditations, mindfulness exercises, and educational content.

### 4. Practice Mindfulness During Routine Tasks

- **Mindful Hygiene:** Bring mindfulness to activities such as brushing your teeth or showering. Focus on the sensations and actions involved, and be present during the process.
- **Mindful Commuting:** Use your commute as an opportunity to practice mindfulness. If you're driving, concentrate on the feel of the steering wheel and the road. If you're using public transport, practice mindful breathing or listen to a calming podcast.

## 5. Create Mindfulness Rituals

- **Morning Routine:** Start your day with a mindfulness practice, such as a short meditation, mindful stretching, or setting intentions for the day.
- **Evening Routine:** End your day with a mindfulness practice, like reflecting on your day, practicing gratitude, or a short meditation before bed.

## 6. Engage in Mindful Movement

- **Yoga:** Incorporate yoga into your routine to combine physical movement with mindfulness. Focus on your breath and body sensations during each pose.
- **Tai Chi:** Practice Tai Chi, which emphasizes slow, deliberate movements and mindful awareness. This can be a calming way to integrate mindfulness into your physical exercise routine.

## 7. Practice Gratitude and Reflection

- **Gratitude Journaling:** Maintain a gratitude journal where you regularly write down things you're thankful for. Reflecting on positive aspects of your life can enhance your mindfulness practice.
- **Mindful Reflection:** Take a few moments each day to reflect on your experiences, emotions, and thoughts. Acknowledge them without judgment and use this reflection to foster self-awareness.

## 8. Attend Mindfulness Workshops or Classes

- **Local Classes:** Look for local mindfulness workshops or classes that can provide structured guidance and support.
- **Online Courses:** Explore online courses and webinars that focus on mindfulness practices and techniques.

## Conclusion

Incorporating mindfulness into your daily life involves making small, consistent efforts to focus on the present moment and engage fully in each experience. By integrating mindfulness practices into routine activities, using mindfulness resources, and creating daily rituals, you can cultivate a greater sense of awareness, calm, and well-being. Remember, mindfulness is a skill that improves with practice, so be patient and persistent in your efforts.

- **Chapter 11: What to Expect in Therapy**
- **Different therapeutic approaches**
- **, building rapport,**
- **communication**

## What to Expect in Therapy

Understanding what to expect in therapy can help you feel more comfortable and prepared for your sessions. Therapy is a collaborative process where you work with a mental health professional to address and manage various emotional and psychological concerns. Here's a breakdown of different therapeutic approaches, building rapport, and effective communication in therapy.

### Different Therapeutic Approaches

1. **Cognitive Behavioral Therapy (CBT):**
   - **Focus:** Identifying and changing negative thought patterns and behaviors.
   - **Methods:** Uses techniques like cognitive restructuring, behavioral activation, and exposure therapy.
   - **Expectations:** Expect to work on setting specific goals, tracking your thoughts and behaviors, and practicing new coping skills.
2. **Psychodynamic Therapy:**
   - **Focus:** Exploring unconscious processes and past experiences to understand current behavior.
   - **Methods:** Uses techniques like free association, dream analysis, and examining transference and countertransference.
   - **Expectations:** Expect to delve into past experiences and unconscious motivations and explore their impact on current relationships and behavior.
3. **Humanistic Therapy:**
   - **Focus:** Promoting personal growth and self-actualization through a non-judgmental and empathetic approach.
   - **Methods:** Uses techniques like client-centered therapy, existential therapy, and gestalt therapy.

- o **Expectations:** Expect a focus on self-exploration, personal values, and achieving a greater sense of self-awareness and fulfillment.

4. **Dialectical Behavior Therapy (DBT):**
   - o **Focus:** Combining cognitive-behavioral techniques with mindfulness practices to manage intense emotions.
   - o **Methods:** Includes skills training in areas such as mindfulness, distress tolerance, emotional regulation, and interpersonal effectiveness.
   - o **Expectations:** Expect structured sessions, homework assignments, and skill-building exercises to help manage emotions and improve relationships.

5. **Family Therapy:**
   - o **Focus:** Addressing family dynamics and improving communication and relationships within the family unit.
   - o **Methods:** Uses techniques like systemic thinking, role-playing, and exploring family roles and patterns.
   - o **Expectations:** Expect to work on family interactions, communication strategies, and resolving conflicts together as a unit.

6. **Group Therapy:**
   - o **Focus:** Providing support and feedback in a group setting, often facilitated by one or more therapists.
   - o **Methods:** Includes sharing experiences, discussing issues, and receiving feedback from peers.
   - o **Expectations:** Expect to interact with others facing similar issues, share experiences, and learn from the group's collective insights and support.

7. **Couples Therapy:**
   - o **Focus:** Improving communication, resolving conflicts, and enhancing intimacy between partners.
   - o **Methods:** Uses techniques such as communication skills training, conflict resolution strategies, and exploring relational dynamics.
   - o **Expectations:** Expect to work on relationship issues together, improve communication, and address conflicts constructively.

## Building Rapport

### Importance:

- Building rapport is essential for creating a trusting and effective therapeutic relationship. It helps you feel comfortable and open during sessions.

**Tips for Building Rapport:**

- **Be Open and Honest:** Share your thoughts, feelings, and concerns openly. Transparency helps build trust and allows the therapist to understand you better.
- **Communicate Your Needs:** Let the therapist know what you need from the therapy process and discuss any concerns or preferences you have.
- **Be Patient:** Building rapport takes time. Allow yourself and the therapist time to develop a comfortable and effective working relationship.
- **Provide Feedback:** Give feedback about what is or isn't working for you in therapy. This helps the therapist adjust their approach to better meet your needs.

**Effective Communication**

**Importance:**

- Effective communication in therapy ensures that both you and the therapist are on the same page and working towards your goals.

**Tips for Effective Communication:**

- **Set Goals:** Discuss and set clear goals for therapy. This helps focus sessions and track progress.
- **Be Specific:** When describing issues or experiences, be as specific and detailed as possible. This provides the therapist with a clearer understanding of your situation.
- **Ask Questions:** If you're unsure about something or need clarification, don't hesitate to ask questions. Understanding the therapy process and techniques can enhance your engagement.
- **Express Emotions:** Share your emotional responses and experiences openly. This helps the therapist understand your feelings and tailor the approach to suit you.

## Conclusion

Understanding what to expect in therapy, including different therapeutic approaches, building rapport, and practicing effective communication, can help make the therapy process more productive and comfortable. Each therapeutic approach has its own methods and focuses, so finding the right fit is important. Building a strong therapeutic relationship and maintaining open communication with your therapist are key components to achieving your goals and gaining the most from your therapy experience.

- **Chapter 12: Medication and Alternative Treatments**
- **Understanding medication,**
- **complementary therapies**

## Medication and Alternative Treatments

When addressing mental health issues, medication and alternative treatments can play significant roles. Understanding both options, including their benefits and limitations, can help you make informed decisions about your treatment plan. Here's a comprehensive overview:

**Understanding Medication**

**1. Types of Medications**

- **Antidepressants:**
    - **SSRIs (Selective Serotonin Reuptake Inhibitors):** Examples include fluoxetine (Prozac) and sertraline (Zoloft). They increase serotonin levels in the brain and are commonly prescribed for depression and anxiety.
    - **SNRIs (Serotonin-Norepinephrine Reuptake Inhibitors):** Examples include venlafaxine (Effexor) and duloxetine (Cymbalta). They affect both serotonin and norepinephrine levels and are used for depression, anxiety, and some types of pain.
    - **Tricyclic Antidepressants (TCAs):** Examples include amitriptyline and nortriptyline (Pamelor). They are used less frequently due to side effects but can be effective for severe depression and chronic pain.
    - **MAOIs (Monoamine Oxidase Inhibitors):** Examples include phenelzine (Nardil) and tranylcypromine (Parnate). They are effective for certain types of depression but require dietary restrictions.
- **Anxiolytics:**
    - **Benzodiazepines:** Examples include diazepam (Valium) and lorazepam (Ativan). They are used for short-term relief of severe anxiety but can be addictive and are generally not recommended for long-term use.

- o **Non-benzodiazepine Anxiolytics:** Examples include buspirone (Buspar). They are used for chronic anxiety and have a lower risk of dependency.
- **Antipsychotics:**
  - o **Typical Antipsychotics:** Examples include haloperidol (Haldol). They are used for schizophrenia and other psychotic disorders but can have significant side effects.
  - o **Atypical Antipsychotics:** Examples include risperidone (Risperdal) and olanzapine (Zyprexa). They are used for schizophrenia, bipolar disorder, and sometimes for severe depression.
- **Mood Stabilizers:**
  - o **Lithium:** Often used for bipolar disorder to stabilize mood swings.
  - o **Anticonvulsants:** Examples include valproate (Depakote) and lamotrigine (Lamictal). They can be effective for mood stabilization in bipolar disorder.
- **Stimulants:**
  - o **Examples include methylphenidate (Ritalin) and amphetamine salts (Adderall).** They are commonly prescribed for attention-deficit/hyperactivity disorder (ADHD) and can help improve focus and impulse control.

## 2. Benefits and Risks

- **Benefits:**
  - o Medications can effectively manage symptoms, improve quality of life, and restore functionality.
  - o They can be a critical part of treatment, especially when combined with therapy and lifestyle changes.

- **Risks:**
  - o Side effects vary by medication and can include weight gain, sexual dysfunction, drowsiness, and more.
  - o Long-term use may lead to dependency or require ongoing monitoring.
  - o It is important to work with a healthcare provider to find the right medication and dosage.

## 3. Working with Your Healthcare Provider

- **Regular Check-ins:** Schedule regular appointments to monitor progress and side effects.
- **Communication:** Discuss any concerns or side effects with your provider. Adjustments to dosage or medication may be necessary.
- **Consistency:** Take medications as prescribed and do not stop or alter dosages without consulting your provider.

**Complementary and Alternative Therapies**

## 1. Complementary Therapies

- **Mindfulness and Meditation:**
  - Techniques such as mindfulness meditation, progressive muscle relaxation, and guided imagery can help reduce stress and improve mental well-being.
  - Regular practice can enhance emotional regulation and support traditional treatments.
- **Yoga and Tai Chi:**
  - These practices combine physical movement with mindfulness and can improve stress management, mood, and physical health.
- **Acupuncture:**
  - Involves inserting thin needles into specific points on the body. Some studies suggest it may help with anxiety, depression, and pain management.
- **Nutritional Supplements:**
  - Supplements such as omega-3 fatty acids, vitamin D, and certain herbs (e.g., St. John's Wort for depression) can support mental health. Consult with a healthcare provider before starting any supplements.
  -

## 2. Alternative Therapies

- **Herbal Remedies:**
  - **St. John's Wort:** Used for mild to moderate depression but can interact with other medications.
  - **Kava:** Used for anxiety but can have liver-related side effects.

- **Aromatherapy:**
  - Uses essential oils (e.g., lavender, chamomile) for relaxation and stress relief. Can be used in diffusers or topical applications.

- **Homeopathy:**
    - Involves using highly diluted substances to stimulate the body's healing processes. Its efficacy is debated, and it is often considered complementary rather than a primary treatment.

### 3. Integrating Therapies

- **Consultation:** Always consult with a healthcare provider before starting complementary or alternative treatments, especially if you are taking medication.
- **Combination Approach:** Integrating these therapies with traditional treatments can provide a holistic approach to mental health.
- **Personalization:** Choose therapies that resonate with you and align with your health needs and preferences.

## Conclusion

Medication and alternative treatments offer various ways to address mental health concerns. Medications can be highly effective but may come with side effects, so it's essential to work closely with your healthcare provider. Complementary and alternative therapies can support mental health and enhance well-being when used in conjunction with traditional treatments. Always consult with healthcare professionals to develop a personalized and safe treatment plan that meets your needs.

What are some mindfulness apps?

There are several mindfulness apps available that offer guided meditations, mindfulness practices, and tools to help integrate mindfulness into your daily routine. Here are some popular and well-regarded mindfulness apps:

## 1. Headspace

- **Features:**
    - Guided meditations and mindfulness exercises.
    - Sleep aids and relaxation techniques.
    - Courses on stress, anxiety, focus, and more.
    - Personal progress tracking and reminders.
- **Pros:**
    - User-friendly interface.
    - Extensive library of meditation sessions and courses.

- ○ Good for beginners and experienced users alike.
- **Cons:**
  - ○ Some features require a subscription for full access.

## 2. Calm

- **Features:**
  - ○ Guided meditations and breathing exercises.
  - ○ Sleep stories and relaxation music.
  - ○ Daily Calm: A daily meditation session.
  - ○ Tools for managing stress and improving focus.
- **Pros:**
  - ○ Diverse range of content, including sleep aids.
  - ○ Attractive, easy-to-navigate design.
  - ○ High-quality sleep stories and soothing sounds.
- **Cons:**
  - ○ Premium content requires a subscription.

## 3. Insight Timer

- **Features:**
  - ○ Extensive library of free guided meditations and music tracks.
  - ○ Meditation timer with customizable bells.
  - ○ Courses on various mindfulness topics.
  - ○ Community features to connect with other users.
- **Pros:**
  - ○ Large collection of free content.
  - ○ Community and social features.
  - ○ Wide range of meditation practices and instructors.
- **Cons:**
  - ○ User interface can be less polished compared to some paid apps.

## 4. 10% Happier

- **Features:**
  - ○ Practical meditation and mindfulness courses.
  - ○ Content designed for skeptics and beginners.
  - ○ Expert interviews and real-world advice on mindfulness.
  - ○ Daily meditation practices and progress tracking.

- **Pros:**
  - Focused on practical, evidence-based approaches.
  - Features well-known meditation teachers and experts.
  - Includes podcasts and articles on mindfulness.
- **Cons:**
  - Subscription required for full access.

## 5. Simple Habit

- **Features:**
  - Short, guided meditations designed for busy schedules.
  - Sessions focused on specific issues like stress, sleep, and productivity.
  - Personalized meditation recommendations.
- **Pros:**
  - Short sessions ideal for quick breaks during the day.
  - Variety of topics and practical guidance.
  - User-friendly interface.
- **Cons:**
  - Premium subscription needed for full access to all features.

## 6. Breathe

- **Features:**
  - Guided meditations, sleep stories, and relaxation techniques.
  - Tools for stress management and personal growth.
  - Daily mindfulness practices and goal-setting features.
- **Pros:**
  - Variety of content including meditation, sleep aids, and personal development.
  - Accessible for beginners and experienced users.
- **Cons:**
  - Subscription required for full access.

## 7. Smiling Mind

- **Features:**
  - Mindfulness programs tailored for different age groups, including children and adolescents.
  - Evidence-based programs developed in collaboration with psychologists.
  - Daily mindfulness exercises and progress tracking.

- **Pros:**
    - Tailored programs for various age groups.
    - Free to use with optional premium features.
- **Cons:**
    - Limited content compared to some other apps.

## 8. MyLife (formerly Stop, Breathe & Think)

- **Features:**
    - Check-in feature to assess mood and emotions.
    - Personalized meditation and mindfulness exercises based on your current state.
    - Emotional check-ins and progress tracking.
- **Pros:**
    - Personalized approach based on mood and emotions.
    - Variety of mindfulness practices and tools.
- **Cons:**
    - Some features require a subscription.

## Conclusion

Mindfulness apps can be a great way to start or deepen your mindfulness practice. They offer various features such as guided meditations, sleep aids, and stress management tools. Many apps provide both free and premium content, so you can explore different options to find the one that best fits your needs and preferences.

### Can mindfulness help with chronic pain?

Yes, mindfulness can be beneficial for managing chronic pain. While it may not eliminate pain entirely, mindfulness can help individuals cope with pain more effectively by altering their relationship with it and reducing the emotional and psychological distress associated with it. Here's how mindfulness can help with chronic pain:

# 1. Understanding Mindfulness in Pain Management

**Mindfulness** involves paying focused, non-judgmental attention to the present moment. In the context of pain management, mindfulness helps individuals become more aware of their bodily sensations and emotions without becoming overwhelmed by them.

## 2. Benefits of Mindfulness for Chronic Pain

### 1. Reduces Pain Perception:

- **Mechanism:** Mindfulness practices can alter the way pain is perceived by the brain. By focusing on the present moment and observing pain without judgment, individuals can reduce the intensity of their pain experience.
- **Research:** Studies have shown that mindfulness can lead to changes in brain areas associated with pain perception, reducing the subjective experience of pain.

### 2. Enhances Emotional Regulation:

- **Mechanism:** Mindfulness helps individuals manage the emotional responses associated with pain, such as frustration, anxiety, and depression. By cultivating a non-reactive awareness, people can experience less distress and more acceptance.
- **Research:** Mindfulness-based interventions have been found to reduce anxiety, depression, and emotional distress in people with chronic pain.

### 3. Improves Coping Skills:

- **Mechanism:** Mindfulness teaches coping strategies such as deep breathing, body scanning, and mindful movement. These techniques can help manage pain flare-ups and improve overall resilience.
- **Research:** Mindfulness-based programs have been shown to improve coping skills and increase pain tolerance in chronic pain patients.

### 4. Promotes Relaxation and Reduces Stress:

- **Mechanism:** Mindfulness practices, such as meditation and relaxation techniques, help activate the body's relaxation response, reducing stress and muscle tension that can exacerbate pain.

- **Research:** Mindfulness-based stress reduction (MBSR) programs have demonstrated significant benefits in reducing stress and pain in various populations.

## 5. Encourages a Positive Mindset:

- **Mechanism:** By fostering a non-judgmental and compassionate attitude towards pain, mindfulness helps individuals adopt a more positive and accepting mindset, reducing the overall impact of pain on their quality of life.
- **Research:** Mindfulness can enhance overall well-being and quality of life by promoting a more balanced and accepting attitude towards pain.

# 3. Mindfulness Techniques for Chronic Pain

## 1. Body Scan Meditation:

- **Description:** A guided practice that involves mentally scanning the body from head to toe, focusing on areas of tension and pain without judgment.
- **Benefits:** Helps increase body awareness and acceptance, and can reduce muscle tension and pain perception.

## 2. Mindful Breathing:

- **Description:** Involves focusing on the breath, observing each inhalation and exhalation with full attention.
- **Benefits:** Helps calm the nervous system, reduce stress, and manage pain more effectively.

## 3. Mindful Movement:

- **Description:** Includes gentle movements or exercises such as yoga or tai chi, performed with mindful awareness.
- **Benefits:** Can improve flexibility, reduce stiffness, and help manage pain through physical activity.

## 4. Loving-Kindness Meditation:

- **Description:** A practice that involves sending thoughts of kindness and compassion to oneself and others.
- **Benefits:** Helps foster a compassionate attitude towards oneself and pain, reducing emotional distress and enhancing overall well-being.

## 5. Pain-Acceptance Strategies:

- **Description:** Techniques that focus on accepting pain rather than resisting or avoiding it, such as using mindfulness to observe pain sensations without judgment.
- **Benefits:** Helps change the relationship with pain, reducing the mental struggle and suffering associated with it.

## 4. Incorporating Mindfulness into Daily Life

### 1. Regular Practice:

- Dedicate time each day to mindfulness practices. Even short periods of 5-10 minutes can be effective.

### 2. Integration into Routine:

- Use mindfulness techniques during daily activities, such as mindful eating, walking, or during moments of pain flare-ups.

### 3. Seek Professional Guidance:

- Consider participating in a mindfulness-based program or working with a therapist trained in mindfulness-based approaches to chronic pain.

## 5. Limitations and Considerations

### 1. Individual Differences:

- Mindfulness may not work equally well for everyone. It's important to find the right approach and techniques that work for your specific needs.

### 2. Complementary Approach:

- Mindfulness should be considered as a complementary approach rather than a replacement for medical treatments or therapies. It's best used in conjunction with other pain management strategies.

### 3. Professional Support:

- Consult with healthcare professionals before starting new practices, especially if you have any health conditions or are on medication.

## Conclusion

Mindfulness can be a valuable tool for managing chronic pain by altering the way you experience and respond to pain. Through practices such as body scan meditation, mindful breathing, and acceptance strategies, individuals can gain better control over their pain experience, reduce emotional distress, and improve overall quality of life. As with any approach, it is important to integrate mindfulness as part of a comprehensive pain management plan and seek professional guidance to tailor practices to your individual needs.

**What are the best meditation techniques?**

Meditation techniques can vary widely, each offering unique benefits and approaches to enhancing mental well-being, relaxation, and self-awareness. Here are some of the best and most widely practiced meditation techniques:

## 1. Mindfulness Meditation

**Description:**

- Focuses on being present in the moment, observing thoughts, sensations, and emotions without judgment.

**How to Practice:**

- Find a quiet place to sit comfortably.
- Close your eyes and focus on your breath, noticing the inhalation and exhalation.
- When your mind wanders, gently bring your attention back to your breath or present sensations.

**Benefits:**

- Enhances awareness and concentration.
- Reduces stress, anxiety, and symptoms of depression.
- Improves emotional regulation and resilience.

## 2. Guided Meditation

**Description:**

- Involves following verbal instructions from a teacher or recording, often leading you through a visual journey or relaxation process.

**How to Practice:**

- Use a guided meditation app or recording.
- Follow the instructions, which might include visualization, relaxation techniques, or body scans.

**Benefits:**

- Useful for beginners who need direction.
- Can address specific goals like stress reduction, sleep improvement, or self-compassion.
- Often incorporates elements of mindfulness and relaxation.

## 3. Loving-Kindness Meditation (Metta)

**Description:**

- Focuses on cultivating feelings of compassion and love towards oneself and others.

**How to Practice:**

- Sit comfortably and close your eyes.
- Begin by focusing on yourself, silently repeating phrases like "May I be happy," "May I be healthy," etc.
- Gradually extend these wishes to others: loved ones, acquaintances, and even those with whom you have conflicts.

**Benefits:**

- Enhances emotional well-being and compassion.
- Reduces negative emotions and increases positive feelings.
- Can improve relationships and social connections.

## 4. Body Scan Meditation

**Description:**

- Involves mentally scanning the body for sensations, tension, or discomfort, and cultivating awareness of physical sensations.

**How to Practice:**

- Lie down or sit comfortably.
- Start at the top of your head and slowly bring your attention to each part of your body, noticing any sensations or tension.
- Use your breath to help release tension and promote relaxation in each area.

**Benefits:**

- Increases body awareness.
- Helps release physical and mental tension.
- Can be particularly useful for managing stress and chronic pain.

## 5. Transcendental Meditation (TM)

**Description:**

- A mantra-based meditation technique involving the repetition of a specific sound or word (mantra) to achieve a deep state of relaxation.

**How to Practice:**

- Sit comfortably with your eyes closed.
- Silently repeat your assigned mantra.
- Allow thoughts to come and go while gently returning your focus to the mantra.

**Benefits:**

- Promotes deep relaxation and stress reduction.
- Can improve overall mental clarity and emotional stability.
- Often practiced in short, twice-daily sessions.

## 6. Zen Meditation (Zazen)

**Description:**

- A form of seated meditation practiced in Zen Buddhism, emphasizing posture and breath awareness.

**How to Practice:**

- Sit cross-legged or in a chair with a straight back.
- Focus on your breath or simply observe your thoughts without engagement.
- Maintain a posture of alert relaxation, often with eyes half-open.

**Benefits:**

- Enhances concentration and mindfulness.
- Promotes a deep sense of calm and presence.
- Encourages insight and self-awareness.

## 7. Vipassana Meditation

**Description:**

- An insight meditation technique rooted in Buddhist traditions, focusing on the awareness of bodily sensations and their impermanence.

**How to Practice:**

- Sit in a comfortable position and focus on the sensations of the body.
- Observe physical sensations, thoughts, and emotions as they arise and pass away.
- Practice non-attachment and equanimity towards these sensations.

**Benefits:**

- Deepens self-awareness and insight into the nature of suffering.
- Enhances emotional regulation and mental clarity.
- Often practiced in intensive retreats for deeper experiences.

## 8. Chanting Meditation

**Description:**

- Involves repeating a specific sound, word, or phrase (mantra) either silently or out loud.

**How to Practice:**

- Choose a mantra or chant (e.g., "Om," "So Hum").
- Repeat the mantra slowly and rhythmically, focusing on the sound and vibration.
- Allow the chant to become a meditative focal point.

**Benefits:**

- Can enhance focus and concentration.
- Promotes relaxation and inner peace.
- Integrates the mind, body, and spirit through sound.

## 9. Movement-Based Meditation

**Description:**

- Includes practices such as Yoga or Tai Chi that combine physical movement with mindfulness.

**How to Practice:**

- Follow a sequence of physical postures or movements with a focus on breath and bodily sensations.
- Maintain awareness of the flow and rhythm of your movements.

**Benefits:**

- Integrates physical exercise with mindfulness.
- Improves flexibility, strength, and balance.
- Enhances overall physical and mental well-being.

## 10. Mantra Meditation

**Description:**

- Involves repeating a specific word, phrase, or sound (mantra) to help focus the mind and achieve a meditative state.

**How to Practice:**

- Choose a mantra that resonates with you (e.g., "peace," "love").

- Repeat the mantra silently or out loud, allowing it to anchor your attention.

**Benefits:**

- Enhances focus and concentration.
- Can promote a deep sense of inner calm and tranquility.
- Often used in conjunction with other meditation techniques.

## Conclusion

The best meditation technique for you depends on your goals, preferences, and experience level. Experimenting with different methods can help you find the one that resonates most with you and best fits your needs. Regular practice, even if for just a few minutes each day, can lead to significant benefits for your mental and emotional well-being.

- Chapter 13: Self-Advocacy and Support Groups (Communicating your needs, finding a support group)

## Self-Advocacy and Support Groups

**Self-advocacy** and participation in **support groups** are crucial components of managing mental health and well-being. They empower individuals to communicate their needs effectively and connect with others who share similar experiences. Here's a guide to understanding and engaging in self-advocacy and support groups:

---

# Self-Advocacy

### 1. Understanding Self-Advocacy

**Definition:**

- Self-advocacy is the ability to speak up for yourself and your needs, make informed decisions about your health and well-being, and take control of your personal and professional life.

**Importance:**

- Helps ensure that your needs and preferences are considered in decisions about your care and life.
- Empowers you to seek appropriate support and resources.
- Enhances your overall sense of control and well-being.

## 2. Communicating Your Needs

### 1. Be Clear and Specific:

- **What to Do:** Articulate your needs and concerns in a clear and specific manner. Avoid vague statements and provide concrete examples.
- **Example:** Instead of saying "I feel stressed," you might say, "I feel overwhelmed by my workload and need support to manage my tasks."

### 2. Practice Active Listening:

- **What to Do:** When communicating with healthcare providers or others, actively listen to their responses and feedback. Engage in a two-way conversation to ensure mutual understanding.
- **Example:** Reflect back what you hear by saying, "It sounds like you're suggesting a different approach. Can you explain how that might work?"

### 3. Know Your Rights:

- **What to Do:** Familiarize yourself with your rights regarding mental health care, workplace accommodations, and other relevant areas. This knowledge empowers you to advocate effectively.
- **Example:** Research legal rights related to mental health in your country or region, such as the right to reasonable accommodations at work.

### 4. Set Boundaries:

- **What to Do:** Establish clear boundaries regarding what you can and cannot do. Communicate these boundaries respectfully and assertively.
- **Example:** If you need time for self-care, you might say, "I need to take a break from work to manage my stress. I'll be unavailable for the next hour."

### 5. Seek Support and Resources:

- **What to Do:** Don't hesitate to seek help from professionals, friends, or family when advocating for yourself. Support can provide valuable insights and reinforcement.
- **Example:** Consult with a counselor or advocate to develop strategies for communicating your needs effectively.

# Finding and Participating in Support Groups

## 1. Understanding Support Groups

**Definition:**

- Support groups are gatherings of individuals who share similar experiences or challenges, providing mutual support, understanding, and advice.

**Benefits:**

- Offers emotional support and a sense of belonging.
- Provides a platform to share experiences and coping strategies.
- Can help reduce feelings of isolation and stigma.

## 2. Finding a Support Group

### 1. Identify Your Needs:

- **What to Do:** Determine what type of support group would best meet your needs. Consider whether you need support for mental health issues, chronic illness, or other specific challenges.
- **Example:** If you're managing anxiety, look for a support group focused on anxiety and stress management.

### 2. Search Online:

- **What to Do:** Use online resources to find support groups. Websites like Meetup, Facebook Groups, or specialized platforms can help you locate groups in your area.
- **Example:** Search for "anxiety support groups near me" or "chronic pain support group online."

### 3. Consult Healthcare Providers:

- **What to Do:** Ask your healthcare provider or therapist for recommendations on support groups. They often have connections with local or online groups.
- **Example:** Request a referral to a support group from your mental health professional.

**4. Reach Out to Organizations:**

- **What to Do:** Contact organizations or non-profits related to your area of need. Many offer support groups or can direct you to relevant resources.
- **Example:** Contact organizations like the National Alliance on Mental Illness (NAMI) or the American Chronic Pain Association for group recommendations.

**5. Evaluate Group Fit:**

- **What to Do:** Attend a few meetings to see if the group aligns with your needs and preferences. Assess the group's atmosphere, leadership, and focus.
- **Example:** Evaluate whether the group's approach and members' experiences resonate with you and contribute positively to your well-being.

**3. Participating Effectively in Support Groups**

**1. Be Open and Honest:**

- **What to Do:** Share your experiences and challenges openly. Authenticity fosters a supportive environment and helps build trust with other members.
- **Example:** Express your feelings and concerns honestly, even if it feels uncomfortable.

**2. Respect Others:**

- **What to Do:** Listen actively and respect others' experiences and viewpoints. Avoid interrupting or dismissing others' contributions.
- **Example:** Practice active listening and offer supportive feedback rather than offering unsolicited advice.

**3. Set Personal Goals:**

- **What to Do:** Identify personal goals for participating in the group, such as gaining coping strategies or building a support network.
- **Example:** Set a goal to learn one new coping technique or to connect with one other member each month.

**4. Maintain Confidentiality:**

- **What to Do:** Respect the confidentiality of group discussions. Keep what is shared in the group private and confidential.

- **Example:** Avoid discussing specific details or personal stories shared in the group outside of the meetings.

**5. Take Responsibility for Your Participation:**

- **What to Do:** Be proactive in attending meetings and engaging in discussions. Your active participation contributes to the group's effectiveness and support network.
- **Example:** Commit to attending regularly and contribute to discussions or activities as needed.

---

## Conclusion

**Self-advocacy** and participation in **support groups** are essential for managing mental health and well-being. Effective self-advocacy involves clear communication, knowing your rights, and seeking support. Support groups provide emotional support and shared experiences that can enhance coping and reduce isolation. By engaging in these practices, you can foster a more supportive and empowered approach to managing your mental health and well-being.

### Can you recommend self-care strategies?

Certainly! Self-care is crucial for maintaining mental, emotional, and physical well-being. Here's a comprehensive list of self-care strategies that you can incorporate into your routine to enhance overall health and resilience:

## 1. Physical Self-Care

**1. Exercise Regularly:**

- **What to Do:** Engage in physical activities such as walking, jogging, yoga, or strength training.
- **Benefits:** Improves mood, reduces stress, and enhances physical health.

**2. Prioritize Sleep:**

- **What to Do:** Aim for 7-9 hours of quality sleep each night. Establish a consistent sleep routine and create a restful environment.

- **Benefits:** Boosts mood, cognitive function, and overall health.

### 3. Eat a Balanced Diet:

- **What to Do:** Incorporate a variety of fruits, vegetables, whole grains, lean proteins, and healthy fats into your meals.
- **Benefits:** Supports energy levels, mood stability, and physical health.

### 4. Hydrate:

- **What to Do:** Drink plenty of water throughout the day to stay hydrated.
- **Benefits:** Supports bodily functions, energy levels, and overall health.

### 5. Practice Good Hygiene:

- **What to Do:** Maintain regular personal hygiene routines, such as showering, brushing teeth, and skincare.
- **Benefits:** Promotes physical comfort and self-esteem.

## 2. Emotional Self-Care

### 1. Set Boundaries:

- **What to Do:** Establish clear boundaries with work, relationships, and personal time.
- **Benefits:** Reduces stress and prevents burnout.

### 2. Engage in Relaxation Techniques:

- **What to Do:** Practice mindfulness, meditation, or deep breathing exercises.
- **Benefits:** Reduces stress, improves emotional regulation, and promotes relaxation.

### 3. Seek Support:

- **What to Do:** Reach out to friends, family, or a mental health professional for support and guidance.
- **Benefits:** Provides emotional support, reduces feelings of isolation, and offers perspective.

**4. Practice Self-Compassion:**

- **What to Do:** Treat yourself with kindness and understanding, especially during difficult times.
- **Benefits:** Enhances self-esteem and reduces self-criticism.

**5. Engage in Activities You Enjoy:**

- **What to Do:** Spend time doing hobbies or activities that bring you joy and satisfaction.
- **Benefits:** Boosts mood and provides a sense of accomplishment.

## 3. Mental Self-Care

**1. Practice Mindfulness:**

- **What to Do:** Incorporate mindfulness practices such as meditation, body scans, or mindful walking into your daily routine.
- **Benefits:** Improves focus, reduces stress, and enhances overall well-being.

**2. Set Realistic Goals:**

- **What to Do:** Break tasks into manageable steps and set achievable goals.
- **Benefits:** Reduces overwhelm and provides a sense of purpose and achievement.

**3. Manage Stress:**

- **What to Do:** Utilize stress-management techniques such as time management, relaxation exercises, and prioritization.
- **Benefits:** Reduces the impact of stress on your health and well-being.

**4. Engage in Continuous Learning:**

- **What to Do:** Pursue new skills, interests, or knowledge through courses, books, or activities.
- **Benefits:** Enhances cognitive function and provides a sense of accomplishment.

### 5. Practice Gratitude:

- **What to Do:** Keep a gratitude journal or regularly reflect on things you are thankful for.
- **Benefits:** Enhances positivity and overall emotional well-being.

## 4. Social Self-Care

### 1. Foster Meaningful Connections:

- **What to Do:** Build and maintain relationships with friends, family, and community.
- **Benefits:** Provides emotional support, companionship, and a sense of belonging.

### 2. Engage in Social Activities:

- **What to Do:** Participate in social events, group activities, or volunteer opportunities.
- **Benefits:** Strengthens social bonds and provides a sense of community.

### 3. Communicate Openly:

- **What to Do:** Share your thoughts and feelings with trusted individuals.
- **Benefits:** Enhances relationships and reduces emotional burden.

### 4. Seek Professional Help:

- **What to Do:** If needed, consult with a mental health professional for therapy or counseling.
- **Benefits:** Provides expert support and tools for managing mental health challenges.

### 5. Balance Social Time:

- **What to Do:** Ensure that you have a balance between social interactions and alone time.
- **Benefits:** Prevents social burnout and supports personal rejuvenation.

## 5. Spiritual Self-Care

**1. Engage in Reflective Practices:**

- **What to Do:** Spend time in reflection, prayer, or spiritual practices that align with your beliefs.
- **Benefits:** Provides a sense of purpose and connection.

**2. Explore Personal Values:**

- **What to Do:** Reflect on and align your actions with your core values and beliefs.
- **Benefits:** Enhances personal fulfillment and authenticity.

**3. Practice Forgiveness:**

- **What to Do:** Work on forgiving yourself and others for past grievances.
- **Benefits:** Reduces emotional burden and promotes inner peace.

**4. Connect with Nature:**

- **What to Do:** Spend time outdoors and connect with natural environments.
- **Benefits:** Provides relaxation, rejuvenation, and a sense of awe.

**5. Participate in Spiritual Communities:**

- **What to Do:** Engage with groups or communities that share your spiritual or philosophical beliefs.
- **Benefits:** Offers support, connection, and shared experiences.

## Conclusion

Incorporating a variety of self-care strategies into your daily life can help you maintain a balanced and healthy lifestyle. Regularly practicing physical, emotional, mental, social, and spiritual self-care can enhance overall well-being, reduce stress, and improve your quality of life. Adapt these strategies to fit your individual needs and preferences, and remember that self-care is an ongoing process that evolves with your life circumstances.

**Any tips for effective time management?**

Effective time management is essential for maximizing productivity, reducing stress, and achieving a balanced life. Here are some practical tips and strategies to help you manage your time more effectively:

## 1. Set Clear Goals

**1. Define Your Goals:**

- **What to Do:** Establish both short-term and long-term goals for personal and professional areas of your life.
- **Benefits:** Provides direction and purpose, making it easier to prioritize tasks.

**2. Use the SMART Criteria:**

- **What to Do:** Ensure your goals are Specific, Measurable, Achievable, Relevant, and Time-bound.
- **Benefits:** Makes goals clearer and more attainable.

## 2. Prioritize Tasks

**1. Use the Eisenhower Matrix:**

- **What to Do:** Categorize tasks into four quadrants: Urgent and Important, Important but Not Urgent, Urgent but Not Important, Not Urgent and Not Important.
- **Benefits:** Helps prioritize tasks based on their urgency and importance.

**2. Apply the 80/20 Rule (Pareto Principle):**

- **What to Do:** Identify the 20% of tasks that will yield 80% of the results.
- **Benefits:** Focuses your efforts on high-impact activities.

**3. Create a To-Do List:**

- **What to Do:** Write down tasks and prioritize them based on importance and deadlines.
- **Benefits:** Keeps you organized and focused on what needs to be accomplished.

## 3. Plan Your Time

**1. Use a Calendar:**

- **What to Do:** Schedule appointments, deadlines, and tasks using a physical or digital calendar.
- **Benefits:** Provides an overview of your schedule and helps manage time effectively.

## 2. Block Time for Tasks:

- **What to Do:** Allocate specific time blocks for focused work, breaks, and meetings.
- **Benefits:** Encourages dedicated time for tasks and prevents multitasking.

## 3. Set Deadlines:

- **What to Do:** Establish deadlines for tasks and projects, even if they are self-imposed.
- **Benefits:** Creates a sense of urgency and helps you stay on track.

# 4. Manage Distractions

## 1. Identify Distractions:

- **What to Do:** Recognize common distractions such as phone notifications, social media, or noisy environments.
- **Benefits:** Helps you address and minimize sources of interruption.

## 2. Use Technology Wisely:

- **What to Do:** Utilize apps and tools that support time management, such as focus timers or task managers.
- **Benefits:** Enhances productivity and helps you stay focused.

## 3. Create a Dedicated Workspace:

- **What to Do:** Designate a specific area for work or study, separate from leisure spaces.
- **Benefits:** Reduces distractions and improves concentration.

# 5. Optimize Your Workflow

## 1. Apply the Pomodoro Technique:

- **What to Do:** Work for 25 minutes, then take a 5-minute break. After four cycles, take a longer break.
- **Benefits:** Increases productivity and prevents burnout.

### 2. Batch Similar Tasks:

- **What to Do:** Group similar tasks together and complete them in one go.
- **Benefits:** Reduces transition time between different types of tasks and improves efficiency.

### 3. Delegate When Possible:

- **What to Do:** Assign tasks to others if they can be done more effectively by someone else.
- **Benefits:** Frees up your time for higher-priority tasks and responsibilities.

## 6. Maintain Work-Life Balance

### 1. Set Boundaries:

- **What to Do:** Establish clear boundaries between work and personal time.
- **Benefits:** Helps prevent work from encroaching on your personal life and reduces stress.

### 2. Schedule Downtime:

- **What to Do:** Plan regular breaks and leisure activities into your schedule.
- **Benefits:** Prevents burnout and maintains overall well-being.

### 3. Practice Self-Care:

- **What to Do:** Incorporate self-care routines, such as exercise, relaxation, and hobbies.
- **Benefits:** Enhances mental and physical health, contributing to better time management.

## 7. Reflect and Adjust

### 1. Review Your Progress:

- **What to Do:** Regularly assess your progress towards goals and how effectively you're managing your time.
- **Benefits:** Helps you identify what's working and what needs improvement.

### 2. Adjust Your Approach:

- **What to Do:** Make adjustments to your time management strategies based on your reflections and changing circumstances.

- **Benefits:** Ensures continued effectiveness and adaptability in managing your time.

## 3. Celebrate Achievements:

- **What to Do:** Acknowledge and reward yourself for completing tasks and achieving goals.
- **Benefits:** Boosts motivation and reinforces positive time management habits.

## Conclusion

Effective time management involves setting clear goals, prioritizing tasks, planning your time, managing distractions, optimizing your workflow, maintaining work-life balance, and regularly reflecting and adjusting your strategies. By incorporating these tips into your routine, you can enhance productivity, reduce stress, and achieve a more balanced and fulfilling life.

### How can I set effective goals?

Setting effective goals is crucial for achieving personal and professional success. Well-defined goals provide direction, motivation, and a sense of accomplishment. Here's a step-by-step guide on how to set and achieve effective goals:

## 1. Define Your Goals Clearly

### 1. Identify Your Objectives:

- **What to Do:** Reflect on what you want to achieve in various areas of your life, such as career, health, relationships, or personal development.
- **Benefits:** Provides clarity on what you want to focus on and achieve.

### 2. Use the SMART Criteria:

- **What to Do:** Ensure your goals are:
    - **Specific:** Clearly define what you want to accomplish.
    - **Measurable:** Include criteria to track progress and measure success
    - **Achievable:** Set realistic and attainable goals.
    - **Relevant:** Align goals with your broader objectives and values.
    - **Time-bound:** Set a deadline for achieving your goal.
- **Benefits:** Makes goals more structured and actionable.

### 3. Break Down Large Goals:

- **What to Do:** Divide big goals into smaller, manageable tasks or milestones.
- **Benefits:** Makes goals less overwhelming and easier to tackle.

## 2. Develop an Action Plan

### 1. Create a Step-by-Step Plan:

- **What to Do:** Outline specific actions you need to take to achieve each goal.
- **Benefits:** Provides a clear path forward and helps you stay organized.

### 2. Set Priorities:

- **What to Do:** Determine which tasks are most important and need to be completed first.
- **Benefits:** Ensures you focus on high-impact activities.

### 3. Allocate Resources:

- **What to Do:** Identify the resources you need, such as time, money, or support, and plan how to acquire them.
- **Benefits:** Ensures you have what you need to successfully achieve your goals.

## 3. Monitor and Review Progress

### 1. Track Your Progress:

- **What to Do:** Regularly monitor your progress towards achieving your goals. Use tools like checklists, journals, or apps.
- **Benefits:** Helps you stay on track and make necessary adjustments.

### 2. Set Milestones:

- **What to Do:** Establish interim goals or milestones to mark your progress along the way.
- **Benefits:** Provides motivation and a sense of accomplishment as you achieve each milestone.

### 3. Reflect and Adjust:

- **What to Do:** Periodically review your goals and action plan. Assess what's working and what needs adjustment.

- **Benefits:** Ensures your goals remain relevant and achievable.

## 4. Stay Motivated and Accountable

### 1. Set Up Accountability:

- **What to Do:** Share your goals with someone who can provide support and hold you accountable, such as a mentor, coach, or friend.
- **Benefits:** Increases motivation and commitment.

### 2. Reward Yourself:

- **What to Do:** Plan rewards for achieving milestones or completing tasks.
- **Benefits:** Reinforces positive behavior and maintains motivation.

### 3. Visualize Success:

- **What to Do:** Use visualization techniques to imagine achieving your goals and the positive impact it will have on your life.
- **Benefits:** Enhances motivation and focus.

## 5. Maintain Flexibility

### 1. Be Open to Change:

- **What to Do:** Be prepared to adjust your goals and plans as circumstances change.
- **Benefits:** Allows you to adapt and stay on course despite challenges.

### 2. Manage Obstacles:

- **What to Do:** Identify potential obstacles and develop strategies to overcome them.
- **Benefits:** Helps you stay resilient and focused.

### 3. Learn from Setbacks:

- **What to Do:** Use setbacks as learning opportunities. Analyze what went wrong and how you can improve.
- **Benefits:** Builds resilience and enhances problem-solving skills.

## 6. Ensure Goals Align with Your Values

**1. Reflect on Personal Values:**

- **What to Do:** Consider how your goals align with your core values and long-term vision.
- **Benefits:** Ensures your goals are meaningful and fulfilling.

**2. Seek Balance:**

- **What to Do:** Strive for a balance between different areas of your life, such as work, personal development, and relationships.
- **Benefits:** Promotes overall well-being and prevents burnout.

## 7. Use Goal-Setting Tools and Techniques

**1. Vision Boards:**

- **What to Do:** Create a visual representation of your goals and aspirations.
- **Benefits:** Keeps your goals visible and top of mind.

**2. SMART Goals Templates:**

- **What to Do:** Use templates to structure and define your goals according to the SMART criteria.
- **Benefits:** Provides a clear framework for goal-setting.

**3. Goal-Tracking Apps:**

- **What to Do:** Utilize apps designed to track and manage your goals and progress.
- **Benefits:** Offers convenience and helps you stay organized.

## Conclusion

Setting effective goals involves defining clear, specific objectives using the SMART criteria, developing a detailed action plan, and regularly monitoring and reviewing progress. Stay motivated by setting up accountability, rewarding yourself, and visualizing success. Remain flexible to adapt to changes and ensure your goals align with your personal values. By following these strategies, you can set and achieve meaningful goals that contribute to your overall success and satisfaction.

**What are common stress management techniques?**

Managing stress effectively is essential for maintaining mental and physical health. Here are some common and effective stress management techniques:

## 1. Relaxation Techniques

**1. Deep Breathing:**

- **What to Do:** Practice deep, diaphragmatic breathing by inhaling slowly through your nose, holding for a few seconds, and exhaling slowly through your mouth.
- **Benefits:** Reduces stress, calms the nervous system, and promotes relaxation.

**2. Progressive Muscle Relaxation (PMR):**

- **What to Do:** Tense and then slowly release each muscle group in your body, starting from your toes and working up to your head.
- **Benefits:** Reduces muscle tension and promotes a sense of relaxation.

**3. Guided Imagery:**

- **What to Do:** Use guided imagery exercises to visualize peaceful and relaxing scenes, such as a beach or forest.
- **Benefits:** Helps divert focus from stress and induces relaxation.

**4. Meditation:**

- **What to Do:** Engage in mindfulness or meditation practices, focusing on the present moment and letting go of distracting thoughts.
- **Benefits:** Reduces stress, enhances emotional well-being, and improves concentration.

## 2. Physical Activity

**1. Exercise Regularly:**

- **What to Do:** Engage in regular physical activity such as walking, jogging, cycling, or swimming.
- **Benefits:** Releases endorphins, improves mood, and reduces stress levels.

**2. Yoga:**

- **What to Do:** Practice yoga, which combines physical postures, breathing exercises, and meditation.
- **Benefits:** Enhances flexibility, reduces tension, and promotes relaxation.

**3. Tai Chi:**

- **What to Do:** Perform Tai Chi, a gentle form of martial arts focusing on slow, flowing movements and deep breathing.
- **Benefits:** Improves balance, reduces stress, and enhances overall well-being.

## 3. Healthy Lifestyle Choices

**1. Maintain a Balanced Diet:**

- **What to Do:** Eat a diet rich in fruits, vegetables, lean proteins, and whole grains. Avoid excessive caffeine and sugar.
- **Benefits:** Supports overall health and can impact mood and stress levels.

**2. Get Adequate Sleep:**

- **What to Do:** Aim for 7-9 hours of quality sleep each night. Maintain a consistent sleep schedule.
- **Benefits:** Restores energy, improves mood, and enhances the ability to cope with stress.

**3. Stay Hydrated:**

- **What to Do:** Drink plenty of water throughout the day.
- **Benefits:** Supports bodily functions and prevents dehydration-related stress.

### 4. Time Management

**1. Prioritize Tasks:**

- **What to Do:** Use tools like to-do lists or time management apps to prioritize tasks and focus on what's most important.
- **Benefits:** Reduces feelings of being overwhelmed and improves productivity.

**2. Break Tasks into Smaller Steps:**

- **What to Do:** Divide large tasks into smaller, manageable steps and tackle them one at a time.
- **Benefits:** Makes tasks seem less daunting and easier to manage.

**3. Take Regular Breaks:**

- **What to Do:** Incorporate short breaks throughout your day to rest and recharge.
- **Benefits:** Prevents burnout and enhances focus and productivity.

## 5. Cognitive Techniques

**1. Cognitive Restructuring:**

- **What to Do:** Challenge and reframe negative or irrational thoughts to reduce their impact.
- **Benefits:** Helps manage stress by changing the way you perceive and react to stressors.

**2. Mindfulness and Acceptance:**

- **What to Do:** Practice mindfulness to stay present and accept things as they are without judgment.
- **Benefits:** Reduces anxiety and stress by focusing on the present moment.

**3. Problem-Solving Skills:**

- **What to Do:** Develop and use effective problem-solving skills to address stressors proactively.
- **Benefits:** Provides a sense of control and reduces feelings of helplessness.

## 6. Social Support

**1. Connect with Friends and Family:**

- **What to Do:** Spend time with supportive friends and family, and share your feelings and concerns.
- **Benefits:** Provides emotional support and helps reduce stress.

**2. Seek Professional Help:**

- **What to Do:** Consult with a therapist or counselor if stress becomes overwhelming or persistent.
- **Benefits:** Offers expert guidance and support for managing stress and developing coping strategies.

**3. Join Support Groups:**

- **What to Do:** Participate in support groups related to your stressors or interests.
- **Benefits:** Provides a sense of community and shared understanding.

## 7. Hobbies and Leisure Activities

**1. Engage in Hobbies:**

- **What to Do:** Spend time on activities you enjoy, such as reading, painting, gardening, or playing an instrument.
- **Benefits:** Provides relaxation and enjoyment, which helps reduce stress.

**2. Practice Relaxing Activities:**

- **What to Do:** Engage in activities that help you unwind, such as taking a bath, listening to music, or watching a movie.
- **Benefits:** Helps you relax and take a break from stressors.

**3. Spend Time in Nature:**

- **What to Do:** Take walks or spend time outdoors in natural settings.
- **Benefits:** Provides a calming effect and reduces stress levels.

## 8. Self-Care Practices

**1. Practice Self-Compassion:**

- **What to Do:** Treat yourself with kindness and understanding, especially during stressful times.

- **Benefits:** Enhances emotional resilience and reduces self-criticism.

### 2. Set Boundaries:

- **What to Do:** Establish clear boundaries to protect your personal time and reduce stress.
- **Benefits:** Helps manage workload and prevent burnout.

### 3. Engage in Mindfulness:

- **What to Do:** Incorporate mindfulness practices into your daily routine, such as mindful eating or mindful walking.
- **Benefits:** Enhances overall well-being and reduces stress.

## Conclusion

Effectively managing stress involves a combination of relaxation techniques, physical activity, healthy lifestyle choices, time management, cognitive techniques, social support, hobbies, and self-care practices. By incorporating these strategies into your daily routine, you can reduce stress, enhance well-being, and improve your overall quality of life. Experiment with different techniques to find what works best for you and adjust as needed.

**Part 4: Maintaining and Enhancing Wellbeing**

- **Chapter 14: Relapse Prevention Strategies**
- **Identifying triggers,**
- **developing coping mechanisms**

Relapse prevention is a critical component of maintaining recovery from various conditions, including substance abuse, mental health issues, and behavioral changes. Identifying triggers and developing coping mechanisms are essential steps in preventing relapse and maintaining long-term success. Here's a comprehensive guide to effective relapse prevention strategies:

## 1. Identifying Triggers

**1. Self-Awareness:**

- **What to Do:** Reflect on past relapses to identify common situations, feelings, or stressors that led to the relapse.
- **Benefits:** Helps in understanding personal triggers and recognizing patterns.

## 2. Keep a Trigger Journal:

- **What to Do:** Maintain a journal to record instances when you feel the urge to relapse, including the context, emotions, and thoughts involved.
- **Benefits:** Provides insight into specific triggers and helps in tracking progress.

## 3. Recognize Emotional Triggers:

- **What to Do:** Identify emotions such as stress, anxiety, depression, or anger that may contribute to relapse.
- **Benefits:** Helps in addressing emotional states that could lead to relapse.

## 4. Identify Environmental Triggers:

- **What to Do:** Recognize environments or social settings that may trigger cravings or urges, such as places where substance use or unhealthy behaviors occurred.
- **Benefits:** Helps in avoiding or modifying environments that could lead to relapse.

## 5. Social and Relational Triggers:

- **What to Do:** Identify people or social interactions that may influence or trigger a relapse.
- **Benefits:** Allows for better management of social relationships and interactions.

## 2. Developing Coping Mechanisms

### 1. Create a Relapse Prevention Plan:

- **What to Do:** Develop a detailed plan outlining strategies to use when facing triggers or cravings, including emergency contacts and specific actions to take.
- **Benefits:** Provides a structured approach to handling high-risk situations.

## 2. Build a Support Network:

- **What to Do:** Surround yourself with supportive friends, family, or support groups who can offer encouragement and accountability.
- **Benefits:** Provides emotional support and helps in managing triggers.

## 3. Develop Healthy Stress Management Techniques:

- **What to Do:** Practice stress-relief strategies such as exercise, meditation, deep breathing, or engaging in hobbies.
- **Benefits:** Reduces stress, which can be a major trigger for relapse.

## 4. Establish Healthy Routines:

- **What to Do:** Create and stick to a daily routine that includes balanced activities such as work, leisure, and self-care.
- **Benefits:** Provides structure and stability, reducing the likelihood of relapse.

## 5. Set and Monitor Personal Goals:

- **What to Do:** Set realistic, achievable goals and regularly monitor your progress towards these goals.
- **Benefits:** Provides motivation and a sense of purpose, helping to stay focused on recovery.

## 6. Practice Mindfulness and Self-Awareness:

- **What to Do:** Engage in mindfulness practices to stay aware of your thoughts and feelings and recognize early signs of potential relapse.
- **Benefits:** Enhances self-awareness and helps in managing cravings and triggers.

## 7. Learn and Practice Refusal Skills:

- **What to Do:** Develop and practice skills to assertively refuse unhealthy behaviors or substances in tempting situations.
- **Benefits:** Strengthens your ability to resist relapse triggers.

**8. Seek Professional Help:**

- **What to Do:** Work with therapists, counselors, or coaches to address underlying issues and develop coping strategies.
- **Benefits:** Provides expert guidance and support for managing triggers and preventing relapse.

## 3. Building Resilience and Self-Efficacy

**1. Focus on Personal Strengths:**

- **What to Do:** Identify and leverage your personal strengths and resources to support your recovery.
- **Benefits:** Enhances self-confidence and resilience in the face of challenges.

**2. Develop Problem-Solving Skills:**

- **What to Do:** Strengthen your ability to effectively solve problems and handle stressors that could lead to relapse.
- **Benefits:** Equips you with tools to navigate difficult situations without resorting to relapse.

**3. Engage in Continuous Learning:**

- **What to Do:** Educate yourself about your condition, relapse prevention, and recovery strategies.
- **Benefits:** Provides valuable knowledge and skills for maintaining recovery.

## 4. Creating a Relapse Prevention Plan

**1. Identify High-Risk Situations:**

- **What to Do:** List situations that are particularly risky for relapse and develop specific strategies to handle them.
- **Benefits:** Prepares you to manage high-risk scenarios more effectively.

**2. Develop a Support System:**

- **What to Do:** Ensure you have a network of support people, including sponsors, therapists, and support groups.
- **Benefits:** Provides a safety net and accountability.

**3. Create a Crisis Response Plan:**

- **What to Do:** Outline steps to take if you experience a significant craving or stressor, including who to contact and what actions to take.
- **Benefits:** Offers immediate strategies for managing crises and preventing relapse.

### 4. Regularly Review and Adjust the Plan:

- **What to Do:** Periodically review and update your relapse prevention plan based on your experiences and progress.
- **Benefits:** Keeps the plan relevant and effective as circumstances change.

## Conclusion

Relapse prevention involves identifying triggers, developing effective coping mechanisms, building resilience, and creating a structured relapse prevention plan. By understanding and addressing triggers, practicing healthy coping strategies, and utilizing support systems, you can significantly reduce the risk of relapse and maintain long-term recovery. Regularly reviewing and adjusting your strategies ensures that they remain effective and relevant to your evolving needs.

### How can I improve sleep quality?

Improving sleep quality is essential for overall health and well-being. Good sleep enhances cognitive function, emotional stability, and physical health. Here are several strategies to help you improve your sleep quality:

## 1. Establish a Consistent Sleep Routine

### 1. Set a Regular Sleep Schedule:

- **What to Do:** Go to bed and wake up at the same time every day, even on weekends.
- **Benefits:** Regulates your body's internal clock, making it easier to fall asleep and wake up.

### 2. Create a Pre-Sleep Routine:

- **What to Do:** Develop a relaxing pre-sleep routine, such as reading, taking a warm bath, or practicing deep breathing.
- **Benefits:** Signals to your body that it's time to wind down and prepare for sleep.

## 2. Optimize Your Sleep Environment

### 1. Make Your Bedroom Comfortable:

- **What to Do:** Ensure your mattress, pillows, and bedding are comfortable and supportive.
- **Benefits:** Creates a conducive sleep environment.

### 2. Control Room Temperature:

- **What to Do:** Keep your bedroom cool, ideally between 60-67°F (15-19°C).
- **Benefits:** Helps regulate body temperature and promotes restful sleep.

### 3. Minimize Light and Noise:

- **What to Do:** Use blackout curtains or an eye mask to block light and consider earplugs or a white noise machine to reduce noise.
- **Benefits:** Creates a dark and quiet environment that supports better sleep.

### 4. Limit Bedroom Use:

- **What to Do:** Use your bedroom primarily for sleep and intimacy, not for work or watching TV.
- **Benefits:** Strengthens the association between your bedroom and sleep.

## 3. Monitor Your Diet and Caffeine Intake

### 1. Avoid Heavy Meals Before Bed:

- **What to Do:** Refrain from eating large or spicy meals within 2-3 hours before bedtime.
- **Benefits:** Reduces the likelihood of indigestion or discomfort affecting your sleep.

### 2. Limit Caffeine and Nicotine:

- **What to Do:** Avoid consuming caffeine and nicotine in the late afternoon or evening.
- **Benefits:** Prevents these stimulants from interfering with your ability to fall asleep.

### 3. Moderate Alcohol Consumption:

- **What to Do:** Limit alcohol intake, especially close to bedtime.
- **Benefits:** While alcohol may make you feel drowsy, it can disrupt sleep patterns and reduce sleep quality.

## 4. Incorporate Physical Activity

### 1. Exercise Regularly:

- **What to Do:** Engage in regular physical activity, such as walking, jogging, or yoga.
- **Benefits:** Improves sleep quality and helps you fall asleep faster. Aim to exercise at least 30 minutes most days, but avoid vigorous exercise close to bedtime.

### 2. Balance Activity with Rest:

- **What to Do:** Ensure that your exercise routine is balanced with adequate rest and relaxation.
- **Benefits:** Prevents over-exertion, which could negatively impact sleep.

## 5. Manage Stress and Anxiety

### 1. Practice Relaxation Techniques:

- **What to Do:** Use techniques such as deep breathing, progressive muscle relaxation, or meditation to manage stress.
- **Benefits:** Helps calm your mind and prepare your body for restful sleep.

### 2. Address Anxiety and Worry:

- **What to Do:** Consider journaling your thoughts before bed or seeking professional help if anxiety is affecting your sleep.
- **Benefits:** Reduces the mental clutter that can interfere with falling asleep.

### 3. Develop Coping Skills:

- **What to Do:** Implement stress management techniques and coping strategies during the day to reduce nighttime anxiety.
- **Benefits:** Enhances overall resilience and reduces the impact of stress on sleep.

## 6. Limit Screen Time Before Bed

**1. Reduce Exposure to Screens:**

- **What to Do:** Avoid screens (phones, tablets, computers, TV) at least an hour before bed.
- **Benefits:** Reduces exposure to blue light, which can interfere with melatonin production and disrupt sleep.

**2. Use Blue Light Filters:**

- **What to Do:** If you must use screens, consider using blue light filters or settings that reduce blue light exposure.
- **Benefits:** Minimizes the impact of blue light on your sleep-wake cycle.

## 7. Address Sleep Disorders

**1. Recognize Sleep Disorders:**

- **What to Do:** Be aware of symptoms of sleep disorders such as insomnia, sleep apnea, or restless legs syndrome.
- **Benefits:** Early identification allows for timely intervention and treatment.

**2. Seek Professional Help:**

- **What to Do:** Consult with a healthcare provider or sleep specialist if you suspect you have a sleep disorder or if you continue to have difficulty sleeping despite implementing good sleep practices.
- **Benefits:** Provides access to diagnosis, treatment, and tailored strategies for improving sleep.

## 8. Maintain a Healthy Lifestyle

**1. Stay Hydrated:**

- **What to Do:** Drink enough water throughout the day but reduce fluid intake in the evening to minimize nighttime awakenings.
- **Benefits:** Supports overall health and prevents disruptions due to nighttime trips to the bathroom.

**2. Avoid Naps Late in the Day:**

- **What to Do:** If you need to nap, limit it to 20-30 minutes and avoid napping late in the afternoon.
- **Benefits:** Prevents interference with your nighttime sleep routine.

**3. Maintain a Balanced Routine:**

- **What to Do:** Incorporate regular wake-up and bedtime routines, balanced with work, relaxation, and leisure activities.
- **Benefits:** Promotes overall well-being and supports a consistent sleep pattern.

## Conclusion

Improving sleep quality involves establishing a consistent sleep routine, optimizing your sleep environment, managing diet and caffeine intake, incorporating physical activity, and addressing stress and anxiety. By following these strategies and making adjustments as needed, you can enhance your sleep quality and overall health. If difficulties persist, consider seeking professional guidance to address any underlying sleep disorders or challenges.

- **Chapter 15: Setting Realistic Goals**
- **Importance of personalized goals,**
- **SMART goal framework**

Setting realistic goals is a crucial aspect of personal and professional development. It involves defining objectives that are achievable and meaningful, taking into account your individual circumstances, resources, and aspirations. Here's a comprehensive guide on how to set and achieve realistic goals using the SMART framework and emphasizing the importance of personalized goals:

## 1. Importance of Personalized Goals

**1. Align with Personal Values and Interests:**

- **What to Do:** Set goals that reflect your personal values, interests, and passions.
- **Benefits:** Increases motivation, engagement, and satisfaction as you work towards achieving them.

**2. Consider Your Current Situation:**

- **What to Do:** Take into account your current resources, skills, and life circumstances.
- **Benefits:** Ensures that goals are feasible and practical given your current situation.

**3. Tailor Goals to Individual Strengths and Weaknesses:**

- **What to Do:** Set goals that leverage your strengths and address areas where you need improvement.
- **Benefits:** Enhances the likelihood of success by building on what you do well and addressing areas of growth.

**4. Set Goals Based on Personal Aspirations:**

- **What to Do:** Define goals that are meaningful to you personally, rather than those imposed by others.
- **Benefits:** Increases commitment and persistence, as you're more likely to be motivated by goals that resonate with your own desires.

## 2. Using the SMART Goal Framework

The SMART framework provides a structured approach to goal-setting, ensuring that goals are well-defined and actionable. SMART stands for Specific, Measurable, Achievable, Relevant, and Time-bound.

**1. Specific**

- **What to Do:** Define the goal with clear, detailed language. Avoid vague or broad statements.
- **Example:** Instead of "I want to get fit," a specific goal would be "I want to run a 5K race in three months."

**2. Measurable**

- **What to Do:** Establish criteria for measuring progress and success.
- **Example:** "I will run 3 times a week, increasing my distance by 1 mile each week."

**3. Achievable**

- **What to Do:** Ensure the goal is realistic given your current resources, skills, and constraints.

- **Example:** "Given my current fitness level, training for a 5K is achievable within three months with a consistent workout plan."

## 4. Relevant

- **What to Do:** Align the goal with your broader objectives, values, and long-term plans.
- **Example:** "Running a 5K supports my long-term goal of maintaining a healthy lifestyle and improving cardiovascular fitness."

## 5. Time-bound

- **What to Do:** Set a deadline or timeframe for achieving the goal.
- **Example:** "I will complete a 5K race by [specific date], with a training plan starting today."

# 3. Examples of SMART Goals

## 1. Personal Development:

- **Specific:** "I will read one book on leadership each month."
- **Measurable:** "I will track my reading progress by noting the books read and key takeaways."
- **Achievable:** "I have set aside 30 minutes each day for reading."
- **Relevant:** "Enhancing my leadership skills is important for my career advancement."
- **Time-bound:** "I will complete 12 books by the end of the year."

## 2. Health and Fitness:

- **Specific:** "I will lose 10 pounds in 3 months by exercising and eating a balanced diet."
- **Measurable:** "I will track my weight weekly and monitor my food intake using a nutrition app."
- **Achievable:** "I will follow a workout plan of 4 days a week and a meal plan provided by a nutritionist."
- **Relevant:** "Losing weight aligns with my goal of improving my overall health."
- **Time-bound:** "I will achieve this goal within the next 3 months."

### 3. Career Development:

- **Specific:** "I will learn a new programming language by taking an online course."
- **Measurable:** "I will complete the course with a certificate and apply the knowledge in a personal project."
- **Achievable:** "I have enrolled in a course that takes 6 weeks and can dedicate 5 hours per week to it."
- **Relevant:** "Learning this language is crucial for advancing in my career as a software developer."
- **Time-bound:** "I will complete the course and project within 8 weeks."

## 4. Additional Tips for Setting Realistic Goals

### 1. Break Goals into Smaller Steps:

- **What to Do:** Divide larger goals into smaller, manageable tasks.
- **Benefits:** Makes the goal less overwhelming and allows you to track progress more easily.

### 2. Set Priorities:

- **What to Do:** Prioritize goals based on their importance and urgency.
- **Benefits:** Helps focus your efforts on what's most critical and avoids spreading yourself too thin.

### 3. Adjust Goals as Needed:

- **What to Do:** Be flexible and willing to adjust goals based on changing circumstances or new insights.
- **Benefits:** Ensures that goals remain relevant and achievable as situations evolve.

### 4. Celebrate Milestones:

- **What to Do:** Recognize and celebrate progress and milestones achieved along the way.
- **Benefits:** Provides motivation and reinforces positive behavior.

### 5. Seek Accountability:

- **What to Do:** Share your goals with a mentor, friend, or coach who can provide support and hold you accountable.

- **Benefits:** Increases motivation and commitment through external support and encouragement.

## Conclusion

Setting realistic goals involves creating personalized, achievable objectives that align with your values and circumstances. Using the SMART framework—Specific, Measurable, Achievable, Relevant, and Time-bound—ensures that your goals are clearly defined and actionable. By breaking goals into smaller steps, setting priorities, and remaining flexible, you can enhance your ability to achieve them and maintain motivation throughout the process.

### How to handle anxiety effectively?

Handling anxiety effectively involves a combination of strategies and techniques tailored to your individual needs and circumstances. Here's a comprehensive guide to managing anxiety, including practical approaches, coping mechanisms, and therapeutic methods:

## 1. Understanding Anxiety

### 1. Recognize Symptoms:

- **What to Do:** Identify common symptoms such as excessive worry, restlessness, muscle tension, and sleep disturbances.
- **Benefits:** Understanding your symptoms helps in addressing them effectively and seeking appropriate help.

### 2. Understand Triggers:

- **What to Do:** Identify situations, thoughts. or stressors that trigger your anxiety.
- **Benefits:** Awareness of triggers allows for better management and preventive strategies.

## 2. Immediate Coping Techniques

### 1. Deep Breathing Exercises:

- **What to Do:** Practice deep, diaphragmatic breathing by inhaling slowly through your nose, holding, and exhaling slowly through your mouth.
- **Benefits:** Helps calm the nervous system and reduce anxiety symptoms.

## 2. Grounding Techniques:

- **What to Do:** Use grounding exercises such as the 5-4-3-2-1 technique, where you focus on 5 things you can see, 4 you can touch, 3 you can hear, 2 you can smell, and 1 you can taste.
- **Benefits:** Helps bring your attention to the present moment and reduce feelings of overwhelm.

## 3. Progressive Muscle Relaxation (PMR):

- **What to Do:** Tense and then slowly release each muscle group in your body.
- **Benefits:** Reduces physical tension and promotes relaxation.

# 3. Long-Term Strategies

## 1. Cognitive-Behavioral Therapy (CBT):

- **What to Do:** Engage in CBT with a therapist to address negative thought patterns and behaviors contributing to anxiety.
- **Benefits:** Helps reframe distorted thinking and develop healthier coping strategies.

## 2. Mindfulness and Meditation:

- **What to Do:** Practice mindfulness meditation, focusing on the present moment without judgment.
- **Benefits:** Reduces anxiety by promoting relaxation and improving emotional regulation.

## 3. Regular Physical Exercise:

- **What to Do:** Engage in regular physical activity, such as walking, jogging, or yoga.
- **Benefits:** Releases endorphins, improves mood, and reduces anxiety symptoms.

**4. Healthy Lifestyle Choices:**

- **What to Do:** Maintain a balanced diet, get adequate sleep, and avoid excessive caffeine and alcohol.
- **Benefits:** Supports overall mental health and reduces anxiety levels.

**5. Establish a Routine:**

- **What to Do:** Create a structured daily routine to provide stability and predictability.
- **Benefits:** Reduces uncertainty and helps manage anxiety.

## 4. Developing Coping Skills

**1. Set Realistic Goals:**

- **What to Do:** Break larger tasks into smaller, manageable steps and set achievable goals.
- **Benefits:** Reduces feelings of being overwhelmed and provides a sense of accomplishment.

**2. Practice Self-Compassion:**

- **What to Do:** Treat yourself with kindness and understanding, especially during anxious moments.
- **Benefits:** Enhances self-acceptance and reduces self-criticism.

**3. Build Resilience:**

- **What to Do:** Develop problem-solving skills, learn from setbacks, and focus on personal strengths.
- **Benefits:** Increases your ability to cope with stress and anxiety.

## 5. Seeking Professional Help

**1. Therapy Options:**

- **What to Do:** Explore different types of therapy, such as CBT, Acceptance and Commitment Therapy (ACT), or Dialectical Behavior Therapy (DBT).
- **Benefits:** Provides tailored strategies and support for managing anxiety.

**2. Medication:**

- **What to Do:** Consult with a healthcare provider to discuss the potential benefits and risks of medications for anxiety, such as SSRIs or SNRIs.
- **Benefits:** Can help manage symptoms when combined with therapy and lifestyle changes.

### 3. Support Groups:

- **What to Do:** Join a support group for individuals experiencing similar anxiety challenges.
- **Benefits:** Provides a sense of community, shared experiences, and additional coping strategies.

## 6. Practical Daily Strategies

### 1. Journaling:

- **What to Do:** Write down your thoughts, feelings, and experiences related to anxiety.
- **Benefits:** Helps process emotions and identify patterns or triggers.

### 2. Limit Exposure to Stressful Stimuli:

- **What to Do:** Reduce exposure to news, social media, or other sources of stress if they contribute to your anxiety.
- **Benefits:** Minimizes additional stressors and helps maintain emotional balance.

### 3. Engage in Enjoyable Activities:

- **What to Do:** Spend time on activities that bring you joy and relaxation, such as hobbies or spending time with loved ones.
- **Benefits:** Provides positive distractions and enhances mood.

### 4. Practice Time Management:

- **What to Do:** Use time management techniques such as prioritizing tasks and using organizational tools.
- **Benefits:** Reduces feelings of overwhelm and improves productivity.

## 7. Lifestyle and Behavioral Adjustments

### 1. Develop Healthy Boundaries:

- **What to Do:** Set boundaries to protect your time and energy, and learn to say no when necessary.
- **Benefits:** Reduces stress and prevents burnout.

**2. Improve Sleep Hygiene:**

- **What to Do:** Follow good sleep practices, such as maintaining a consistent sleep schedule and creating a relaxing bedtime routine.
- **Benefits:** Enhances sleep quality and overall well-being.

**3. Engage in Relaxation Practices:**

- **What to Do:** Incorporate relaxation techniques such as aromatherapy, listening to calming music, or engaging in creative activities.
- **Benefits:** Promotes relaxation and reduces anxiety.

## Conclusion

Handling anxiety effectively involves a combination of immediate coping techniques, long-term strategies, and lifestyle adjustments. By incorporating practices such as deep breathing, mindfulness, regular exercise, and seeking professional support, you can manage anxiety more effectively and improve your overall quality of life. Personalizing these strategies to fit your individual needs and circumstances is key to achieving lasting relief from anxiety.

- **Chapter 16: Maintaining Healthy Habits**
- **Building routines,**
- **Consistency,**
- **self-compassion**

Maintaining healthy habits is essential for long-term well-being and achieving personal goals. Building effective routines, ensuring consistency, and practicing self-compassion are key components of sustaining these habits. Here's a comprehensive guide on how to develop and maintain healthy habits:

## 1. Building Routines

**1. Start Small:**

- **What to Do:** Begin with manageable changes that you can easily incorporate into your daily life.
- **Benefits:** Reduces the risk of feeling overwhelmed and increases the likelihood of sticking with new habits.

### 2. Create a Structured Plan:

- **What to Do:** Develop a clear plan outlining the habits you want to establish and the specific steps required.
- **Benefits:** Provides a roadmap for implementing and tracking your habits.

### 3. Establish Triggers:

- **What to Do:** Use existing routines or cues as triggers for your new habits. For example, brush your teeth right after your morning exercise.
- **Benefits:** Helps in integrating new habits into your daily routine more seamlessly.

### 4. Set Specific Times:

- **What to Do:** Schedule specific times for your new habits, such as exercising at 7 a.m. or meditating before bed.
- **Benefits:** Adds structure and makes it easier to remember and stick to the habit.

### 5. Use Reminders and Tools:

- **What to Do:** Utilize reminders, alarms, or habit-tracking apps to stay on track.
- **Benefits:** Keeps you accountable and helps reinforce your commitment.

## 2. Ensuring Consistency

### 1. Monitor Progress:

- **What to Do:** Track your progress using a journal, app, or checklist.
- **Benefits:** Provides motivation by showing how far you've come and helps identify patterns or areas for improvement.

### 2. Build Accountability:

- **What to Do:** Share your goals with a friend, family member, or accountability partner.

- **Benefits:** Encourages commitment and provides support and encouragement.

## 3. Reward Yourself:

- **What to Do:** Set up a system of rewards for achieving milestones or maintaining consistency.
- **Benefits:** Reinforces positive behavior and provides motivation to continue.

## 4. Be Flexible:

- **What to Do:** Allow for adjustments to your routine as needed to accommodate changes in your schedule or circumstances.
- **Benefits:** Helps in maintaining habits without feeling rigid or stressed.

## 5. Address Obstacles:

- **What to Do:** Identify potential obstacles and develop strategies to overcome them.
- **Benefits:** Prepares you for challenges and reduces the likelihood of disruption.

## 3. Practicing Self-Compassion

### 1. Be Kind to Yourself:

- **What to Do:** Treat yourself with kindness and understanding, especially when you face setbacks or challenges.
- **Benefits:** Reduces self-criticism and supports a positive mindset.

### 2. Accept Imperfection:

- **What to Do:** Recognize that it's okay to have occasional lapses or setbacks.
- **Benefits:** Helps you stay motivated and resilient, rather than discouraged.

### 3. Focus on Effort, Not Just Outcomes:

- **What to Do:** Appreciate the effort you put into maintaining your habits, regardless of immediate results.
- **Benefits:** Reinforces the value of perseverance and hard work.

**4. Practice Self-Care:**

- **What to Do:** Prioritize activities that nurture your well-being, such as relaxation, hobbies, and spending time with loved ones.
- **Benefits:** Supports overall health and well-being, making it easier to sustain healthy habits.

**5. Reflect on Progress:**

- **What to Do:** Regularly reflect on your progress and acknowledge your achievements.
- **Benefits:** Provides motivation and reinforces positive behavior.

## 4. Building and Maintaining Healthy Habits

**1. Identify Key Habits:**

- **What to Do:** Choose habits that align with your long-term goals and values.
- **Benefits:** Ensures that the habits you work to maintain are meaningful and impactful.

**2. Create a Routine:**

- **What to Do:** Establish a daily or weekly routine that incorporates your key habits.
- **Benefits:** Provides structure and consistency, making it easier to integrate habits into your life.

**3. Stay Flexible:**

- **What to Do:** Be open to adjusting your habits and routines as needed based on changing circumstances.
- **Benefits:** Helps maintain long-term adherence and prevents frustration.

**4. Seek Support:**

- **What to Do:** Engage with support groups, mentors, or professional coaches for guidance and encouragement.
- **Benefits:** Provides additional resources and motivation.

**5. Evaluate and Adjust:**

- **What to Do:** Periodically review your habits and routines to assess their effectiveness and make necessary adjustments.
- **Benefits:** Ensures that your habits continue to serve your goals and well-being.

## Examples of Healthy Habits and Routines

### 1. Morning Routine:

- **Example:** Wake up at 6:30 a.m., meditate for 10 minutes, exercise for 30 minutes, have a healthy breakfast, and plan your day.
- **Benefits:** Sets a positive tone for the day and supports physical and mental well-being.

### 2. Workday Routine:

- **Example:** Start work by prioritizing tasks, take breaks every 90 minutes, stay hydrated, and end the workday with a brief reflection.
- **Benefits:** Enhances productivity and reduces burnout.

### 3. Evening Routine:

- **Example:** Disconnect from screens an hour before bed, read a book, practice relaxation techniques, and go to sleep at the same time each night.
- **Benefits:** Improves sleep quality and supports relaxation.

## Conclusion

Maintaining healthy habits involves building effective routines, ensuring consistency, and practicing self-compassion. By starting small, creating structured plans, monitoring progress, and being kind to yourself, you can establish and sustain habits that contribute to your overall well-being. Flexibility, support, and regular evaluation further enhance your ability to maintain these habits long-term.

### How to improve sleep hygiene?

Improving sleep hygiene is essential for enhancing the quality of your sleep and overall health. Sleep hygiene refers to the practices and habits that promote good sleep quality and help you fall asleep more easily. Here's a comprehensive guide to improving your sleep hygiene:

## 1. Establish a Consistent Sleep Schedule

**1. Set Regular Sleep and Wake Times:**

- **What to Do:** Go to bed and wake up at the same time every day, even on weekends.
- **Benefits:** Regulates your body's internal clock, making it easier to fall asleep and wake up naturally.

**2. Create a Pre-Sleep Routine:**

- **What to Do:** Develop a calming pre-sleep routine, such as reading a book, taking a warm bath, or practicing relaxation techniques.
- **Benefits:** Signals to your body that it's time to wind down and prepare for sleep.

## 2. Optimize Your Sleep Environment

**1. Make Your Bedroom Comfortable:**

- **What to Do:** Ensure your mattress, pillows, and bedding are comfortable and supportive.
- **Benefits:** Enhances physical comfort and promotes restful sleep.

**2. Control Room Temperature:**

- **What to Do:** Keep your bedroom cool, ideally between 60-67°F (15-19°C).
- **Benefits:** Helps regulate body temperature and supports better sleep.

**3. Minimize Light and Noise:**

- **What to Do:** Use blackout curtains or an eye mask to block light and consider earplugs or a white noise machine to reduce noise.
- **Benefits:** Creates a dark and quiet environment conducive to sleep.

**4. Limit Bedroom Use:**

- **What to Do:** Use your bedroom primarily for sleep and intimacy, not for work or watching TV.
- **Benefits:** Strengthens the association between your bedroom and sleep.

## 3. Develop Healthy Lifestyle Habits

**1. Maintain a Balanced Diet:**

- **What to Do:** Avoid heavy meals, caffeine, and alcohol close to bedtime.
- **Benefits:** Prevents discomfort and disruptions in sleep patterns.

**2. Engage in Regular Physical Activity:**

- **What to Do:** Incorporate regular exercise into your routine, but avoid vigorous workouts close to bedtime.
- **Benefits:** Promotes better sleep quality and helps you fall asleep faster.

**3. Avoid Naps Late in the Day:**

- **What to Do:** If you need to nap, limit it to 20-30 minutes and avoid napping in the late afternoon or evening.
- **Benefits:** Prevents interference with your nighttime sleep routine.

## 4. Manage Stress and Anxiety

**1. Practice Relaxation Techniques:**

- **What to Do:** Use techniques such as deep breathing, progressive muscle relaxation, or meditation to manage stress.
- **Benefits:** Helps calm your mind and prepare your body for restful sleep.

**2. Address Anxiety and Worry:**

- **What to Do:** Consider journaling your thoughts before bed or seeking professional help if anxiety affects your sleep.
- **Benefits:** Reduces mental clutter and promotes relaxation.

**3. Create a Worry-Free Zone:**

- **What to Do:** Set aside time earlier in the day to address worries or plan for the next day.
- **Benefits:** Prevents these thoughts from interfering with your ability to fall asleep.

## 5. Limit Exposure to Screens

**1. Reduce Blue Light Exposure:**

- **What to Do:** Avoid screens (phones, tablets, computers, TV) at least an hour before bed. Use blue light filters if necessary.
- **Benefits:** Minimizes disruption to your body's production of melatonin, a hormone that regulates sleep.

**2. Establish Screen-Free Zones:**

- **What to Do:** Keep screens out of the bedroom and avoid using them as a pre-sleep activity.
- **Benefits:** Helps create a more restful environment and routine.

## 6. Create a Comfortable Sleep Routine

**1. Establish a Relaxing Pre-Sleep Activity:**

- **What to Do:** Engage in calming activities such as reading a book, taking a warm bath, or listening to soothing music.
- **Benefits:** Helps signal to your body that it's time to wind down.

**2. Use a Sleep-Inducing Aroma:**

- **What to Do:** Consider using calming scents like lavender through essential oils or scented candles.
- **Benefits:** Promotes relaxation and creates a restful atmosphere.

**3. Maintain a Comfortable Sleep Position:**

- **What to Do:** Find a sleep position that is comfortable for you and supports good posture.
- **Benefits:** Reduces discomfort and supports restful sleep.

## 7. Monitor Your Sleep

**1. Keep a Sleep Diary:**

- **What to Do:** Record your sleep patterns, including bedtimes, wake times, and sleep quality.
- **Benefits:** Helps identify patterns or issues affecting your sleep.

**2. Use Sleep Tracking Devices:**

- **What to Do:** Consider using a sleep tracker or app to monitor your sleep patterns and make adjustments as needed.

- **Benefits:** Provides insights into sleep quality and helps track improvements.

## 8. Seek Professional Help

### 1. Recognize Sleep Disorders:

- **What to Do:** Be aware of symptoms of sleep disorders such as insomnia, sleep apnea, or restless legs syndrome.
- **Benefits:** Early identification allows for timely intervention and treatment.

### 2. Consult a Sleep Specialist:

- **What to Do:** Seek help from a healthcare provider or sleep specialist if you have persistent sleep issues or suspect a sleep disorder.
- **Benefits:** Provides access to diagnosis, treatment, and personalized strategies for improving sleep.

## Conclusion

Improving sleep hygiene involves establishing consistent sleep routines, optimizing your sleep environment, maintaining healthy lifestyle habits, and managing stress and anxiety. By implementing these strategies, you can enhance your sleep quality and overall well-being. If difficulties persist, consulting with a healthcare professional or sleep specialist can provide additional guidance and support.

- **Chapter 17: Living a Fulfilling Life**
- **Finding meaning and purpose,**
- **developing passions**

Living a fulfilling life involves discovering what brings you joy and meaning and aligning your actions with those values and passions. It's about more than just achieving goals; it's about creating a life that feels rich and rewarding on a deep, personal level. Here's a guide to finding meaning and purpose and developing your passions:

## 1. Finding Meaning and Purpose

### 1. Reflect on Core Values:

- **What to Do:** Identify your core values and principles that guide your decisions and actions.
- **How to Do It:** Reflect on moments in your life when you felt most fulfilled or proud. Consider what values were being honored at those times.
- **Benefits:** Helps align your life choices with what truly matters to you.

## 2. Set Meaningful Goals:

- **What to Do:** Establish goals that are not only achievable but also align with your values and long-term aspirations.
- **How to Do It:** Use the SMART goal framework (Specific, Measurable, Achievable, Relevant, Time-bound) and ensure they reflect your personal values.
- **Benefits:** Creates a sense of direction and purpose in your life.

## 3. Engage in Self-Discovery:

- **What to Do:** Explore different aspects of yourself through journaling, self-assessment tools, and mindfulness practices.
- **How to Do It:** Take personality tests, reflect on past experiences, or engage in self-discovery exercises.
- **Benefits:** Increases self-awareness and helps clarify what brings you fulfillment.

## 4. Seek Out New Experiences:

- **What to Do:** Try new activities, hobbies, or roles to explore different aspects of yourself and discover what resonates with you.
- **How to Do It:** Volunteer, take up new hobbies, or travel to new places.
- **Benefits:** Broadens your perspective and helps you discover what you enjoy and value.

## 5. Connect with Others:

- **What to Do:** Build and nurture meaningful relationships and seek connections with people who share your values and passions.
- **How to Do It:** Join clubs, attend community events, or participate in groups related to your interests.
- **Benefits:** Provides support, inspiration, and a sense of belonging.

## 6. Contribute to Something Greater:

- **What to Do:** Find ways to contribute to your community or a cause you care about.
- **How to Do It:** Volunteer, support charitable organizations, or get involved in advocacy.
- **Benefits:** Creates a sense of purpose and fulfillment through making a positive impact.

## 2. Developing Passions

### 1. Explore Interests:

- **What to Do:** Identify and explore your interests and passions.
- **How to Do It:** Make a list of activities you enjoy, research new topics, and experiment with different hobbies.
- **Benefits:** Helps you discover what you are passionate about and how to incorporate these interests into your life.

### 2. Pursue Personal Growth:

- **What to Do:** Engage in continuous learning and personal development to cultivate your passions.
- **How to Do It:** Take courses, read books, or attend workshops related to your interests.
- **Benefits:** Deepens your knowledge and skills, enhancing your enjoyment and engagement.

### 3. Set Passion Projects:

- **What to Do:** Develop projects or goals that align with your passions and interests.
- **How to Do It:** Create a plan for a personal project or initiative that excites you, such as writing a book, starting a blog, or creating art.
- **Benefits:** Provides a sense of accomplishment and joy from pursuing what you love.

### 4. Balance Passion with Practicality:

- **What to Do:** Find a balance between pursuing your passions and addressing practical aspects of your life.
- **How to Do It:** Set realistic expectations and manage your time to incorporate your passions into your daily routine.
- **Benefits:** Ensures that pursuing passions enhances rather than overwhelms your life.

### 5. Reflect and Adjust:

- **What to Do:** Regularly reflect on your passions and how they align with your life goals and values.
- **How to Do It:** Periodically review your progress and adjust your focus based on your evolving interests and life changes.
- **Benefits:** Keeps your pursuits relevant and aligned with your personal growth.

### 6. Share Your Passions:

- **What to Do:** Share your interests and passions with others to build connections and receive support.
- **How to Do It:** Engage in discussions, collaborate on projects, or teach others about your passions.
- **Benefits:** Enhances your sense of community and provides new opportunities for growth and collaboration.

## 3. Integrating Meaning and Passion into Daily Life

### 1. Create a Vision Statement:

- **What to Do:** Develop a personal vision statement that encapsulates your values, purpose, and passions.
- **How to Do It:** Write a statement that reflects your ideal life and what you want to achieve or contribute.
- **Benefits:** Provides clarity and direction for your personal and professional life.

### 2. Prioritize What Matters Most:

- **What to Do:** Make decisions based on your values and passions, focusing on what truly matters to you.
- **How to Do It:** Use your vision statement and goals to guide your choices and actions.
- **Benefits:** Ensures that your time and energy are spent on activities that bring you fulfillment.

### 3. Practice Gratitude:

- **What to Do:** Regularly express gratitude for the aspects of your life that contribute to your sense of fulfillment and joy.
- **How to Do It:** Keep a gratitude journal or make it a part of your daily reflection.

- **Benefits:** Enhances your appreciation of what you have and increases overall satisfaction.

**4. Maintain Flexibility:**

- **What to Do:** Stay open to change and be willing to adapt your goals and passions as you grow and evolve.
- **How to Do It:** Regularly assess your interests and be willing to pivot or explore new directions.
- **Benefits:** Keeps your life dynamic and ensures ongoing growth and fulfillment.

## Conclusion

Living a fulfilling life involves finding meaning and purpose by reflecting on your core values, setting meaningful goals, and exploring new experiences. Developing passions requires discovering and nurturing your interests, pursuing personal growth, and integrating these passions into your daily life. By creating a vision statement, prioritizing what matters most, and practicing gratitude, you can build a life that is rich in purpose and satisfaction. Flexibility and regular reflection ensure that your journey remains aligned with your evolving desires and goals.

**How to balance work and life?**

Balancing work and life is crucial for maintaining overall well-being, productivity, and satisfaction. It involves managing your professional responsibilities while ensuring that you have ample time and energy for personal interests, relationships, and self-care. Here's a comprehensive guide to achieving and maintaining a healthy work-life balance:

## 1. Set Clear Boundaries

**1. Define Work and Personal Time:**

- **What to Do:** Clearly distinguish between work hours and personal time.
- **How to Do It:** Set specific work hours and stick to them. Avoid checking work emails or taking calls outside these hours.
- **Benefits:** Helps create a clear separation between work and personal life.

**2. Create a Dedicated Workspace:**

- **What to Do:** Designate a specific area in your home or office for work.
- **How to Do It:** Set up a separate desk or room for work activities, if possible.
- **Benefits:** Enhances focus during work hours and reduces work encroaching on personal space.

### 3. Communicate Boundaries:

- **What to Do:** Clearly communicate your work boundaries to colleagues, clients, and family members.
- **How to Do It:** Set expectations about availability and response times.
- **Benefits:** Reduces misunderstandings and helps manage expectations.

## 2. Manage Time Effectively

### 1. Prioritize Tasks:

- **What to Do:** Use prioritization techniques to focus on high-impact tasks.
- **How to Do It:** Implement methods like the Eisenhower Matrix or ABC prioritization to categorize tasks.
- **Benefits:** Increases productivity and reduces overwhelm.

### 2. Use Time Management Tools:

- **What to Do:** Utilize tools like calendars, to-do lists, and time-tracking apps.
- **How to Do It:** Schedule your tasks and track how time is spent.
- **Benefits:** Enhances organization and ensures you allocate time efficiently.

### 3. Implement the Pomodoro Technique:

- **What to Do:** Work in focused intervals, typically 25 minutes, followed by a 5-minute break.
- **How to Do It:** Use a timer or Pomodoro app to manage work sessions.
- **Benefits:** Enhances concentration and prevents burnout.

### 4. Delegate and Outsource:

- **What to Do:** Delegate tasks when possible and consider outsourcing tasks that are outside your expertise or time constraints.
- **How to Do It:** Assign tasks to team members or hire external help for specific needs.
- **Benefits:** Reduces workload and frees up time for personal activities.

### 3. Prioritize Self-Care

**1. Incorporate Regular Exercise:**

- **What to Do:** Engage in physical activity regularly.
- **How to Do It:** Schedule exercise sessions into your weekly routine, such as daily walks or gym workouts.
- **Benefits:** Reduces stress, improves mood, and boosts energy levels.

**2. Maintain a Healthy Diet:**

- **What to Do:** Eat a balanced diet to fuel your body and mind.
- **How to Do It:** Plan meals, prepare healthy snacks, and stay hydrated.
- **Benefits:** Enhances overall well-being and supports sustained energy levels.

**3. Get Adequate Sleep:**

- **What to Do:** Prioritize good sleep hygiene and aim for 7-9 hours of quality sleep per night.
- **How to Do It:** Establish a consistent sleep schedule and create a restful environment.
- **Benefits:** Improves cognitive function, mood, and productivity.

**4. Practice Relaxation Techniques:**

- **What to Do:** Incorporate activities that promote relaxation and stress relief.
- **How to Do It:** Engage in practices such as mindfulness, meditation, or deep breathing exercises.
- **Benefits:** Reduces stress and enhances emotional well-being.

## 4. Foster Personal and Professional Relationships

**1. Nurture Relationships:**

- **What to Do:** Invest time in building and maintaining personal relationships.
- **How to Do It:** Schedule regular time with family and friends and engage in meaningful activities together.
- **Benefits:** Strengthens support networks and enriches personal life.

## 2. Seek Support at Work:

- **What to Do:** Communicate with your supervisor or HR about your work-life balance needs.
- **How to Do It:** Discuss flexible work arrangements, such as remote work or adjusted hours.
- **Benefits:** Creates a supportive work environment and addresses work-related stressors.

## 3. Balance Social and Family Life:

- **What to Do:** Ensure that you allocate time for both social activities and family commitments.
- **How to Do It:** Plan social events and family activities in advance to balance your schedule.
- **Benefits:** Maintains a fulfilling social life and strong family bonds.

# 5. Set Realistic Goals and Expectations

## 1. Set Achievable Goals:

- **What to Do:** Establish realistic and attainable goals for both work and personal life.
- **How to Do It:** Use the SMART goal framework to set specific, measurable, achievable, relevant, and time-bound goals.
- **Benefits:** Helps manage expectations and reduces the risk of burnout.

## 2. Learn to Say No:

- **What to Do:** Politely decline additional commitments that you cannot reasonably handle.
- **How to Do It:** Assess your current workload and priorities before agreeing to new tasks or projects.
- **Benefits:** Prevents overextension and maintains balance.

## 3. Reflect and Adjust:

- **What to Do:** Regularly assess your work-life balance and make adjustments as needed.
- **How to Do It:** Evaluate what's working and what isn't, and adjust your routines or boundaries accordingly.
- **Benefits:** Ensures that your approach to balance remains effective and aligned with your needs.

### 6. Integrate Work and Life Seamlessly

**1. Combine Activities:**

- **What to Do:** Find ways to combine work and personal activities when possible.
- **How to Do It:** Schedule work-related tasks that allow for personal interaction, like working from a café or attending professional events with family.
- **Benefits:** Enhances flexibility and makes the most of your time.

**2. Embrace Flexibility:**

- **What to Do:** Be open to flexible work arrangements and adapt your schedule as needed.
- **How to Do It:** Discuss options such as remote work, flexible hours, or job sharing with your employer.
- **Benefits:** Provides better integration of work and personal life.

## Conclusion

Balancing work and life involves setting clear boundaries, managing time effectively, prioritizing self-care, fostering relationships, setting realistic goals, and integrating work and personal activities. By implementing these strategies, you can create a harmonious balance that supports both professional success and personal fulfillment. Regular reflection and adjustment will help you maintain this balance and adapt to changes in your life and work circumstances.

- **Chapter 18: Mental Health and the Future**
- **Continuing support,**
- **self-care for life**

Mental health is a lifelong journey that involves continuous support, self-care, and adaptation to changing circumstances. As we look to the future, maintaining and improving mental health requires an ongoing commitment to understanding, supporting, and nurturing our mental well-being. Here's how to approach mental health and self-care with a long-term perspective:

## 1. Continuing Support

**1. Stay Informed:**

- **What to Do:** Keep yourself updated on the latest research and developments in mental health.
- **How to Do It:** Follow reputable sources, attend workshops or webinars, and read relevant literature.
- **Benefits:** Ensures that you have the most current information to make informed decisions about mental health care.

**2. Build a Support Network:**

- **What to Do:** Cultivate a network of supportive friends, family members, and mental health professionals.
- **How to Do It:** Engage in community groups, maintain regular contact with loved ones, and seek professional guidance as needed.
- **Benefits:** Provides emotional support, practical advice, and helps in managing mental health challenges.

**3. Engage in Regular Therapy:**

- **What to Do:** Consider ongoing therapy or counseling sessions, even when you're not experiencing a crisis.
- **How to Do It:** Schedule periodic check-ins with a therapist or counselor.
- **Benefits:** Offers a safe space for continuous personal growth and mental health maintenance.

**4. Utilize Support Groups:**

- **What to Do:** Participate in support groups for shared experiences and mutual support.
- **How to Do It:** Join groups related to specific issues or general mental wellness, either in-person or online.
- **Benefits:** Provides a sense of community and understanding from those with similar experiences.

**5. Explore New Therapeutic Options:**

- **What to Do:** Stay open to new forms of therapy and treatments as they become available.
- **How to Do It:** Research and consult with healthcare professionals about emerging therapies and techniques.

- **Benefits:** Keeps your approach to mental health care flexible and adaptive.

## 2. Self-Care for Life

### 1. Develop a Personalized Self-Care Plan:

- **What to Do:** Create a self-care plan tailored to your needs and preferences.
- **How to Do It:** Include activities that support physical, emotional, and mental well-being, such as exercise, relaxation, hobbies, and socializing.
- **Benefits:** Ensures that self-care is relevant and effective for your individual needs.

### 2. Practice Mindfulness and Relaxation:

- **What to Do:** Incorporate mindfulness practices and relaxation techniques into your daily routine.
- **How to Do It:** Use methods like meditation, deep breathing, or yoga.
- **Benefits:** Reduces stress and enhances emotional resilience.

### 3. Maintain a Balanced Lifestyle:

- **What to Do:** Focus on a balanced approach to work, leisure, and personal responsibilities.
- **How to Do It:** Schedule regular breaks, set boundaries, and engage in activities that rejuvenate you.
- **Benefits:** Prevents burnout and promotes overall well-being.

### 4. Prioritize Physical Health:

- **What to Do:** Pay attention to physical health as it is closely linked to mental health.
- **How to Do It:** Follow a nutritious diet, exercise regularly, and get adequate sleep.
- **Benefits:** Supports mental health and overall physical well-being.

### 5. Engage in Lifelong Learning:

**What to Do:** Continue learning and growing both personally and professionally.

**How to Do It:** Pursue hobbies, educational opportunities, or skill development.

**Benefits:** Enhances self-esteem and provides a sense of purpose and fulfillment.

### 6. Cultivate Positive Relationships:

- **What to Do:** Build and nurture relationships with people who uplift and support you.
- **How to Do It:** Focus on connecting with positive and encouraging individuals.
- **Benefits:** Provides emotional support and contributes to a fulfilling social life.

### 7. Regularly Reflect and Adjust:

- **What to Do:** Periodically assess your mental health and self-care practices.
- **How to Do It:** Reflect on what's working and make adjustments as necessary.
- **Benefits:** Ensures that your self-care strategies remain effective and aligned with your current needs.

## 3. Addressing Challenges

### 1. Manage Stress Proactively:

- **What to Do:** Develop strategies for managing stress before it becomes overwhelming.
- **How to Do It:** Use techniques such as time management, relaxation exercises, and seeking support.
- **Benefits:** Reduces the impact of stress on your mental health.

### 2. Recognize and Address Burnout:

- **What to Do:** Identify signs of burnout and take steps to address them.
- **How to Do It:** Take breaks, seek professional help, and reassess your workload and responsibilities.

- **Benefits:** Prevents long-term negative effects on mental and physical health.

### 3. Be Prepared for Setbacks:

- **What to Do:** Understand that setbacks may occur and have a plan for addressing them.
- **How to Do It:** Develop coping strategies and seek support when needed.
- **Benefits:** Provides resilience and ensures you can navigate challenges effectively.

## 4. Embracing Change and Adaptation

### 1. Stay Flexible:

- **What to Do:** Adapt your self-care and mental health strategies as your life circumstances change.
- **How to Do It:** Regularly review and adjust your self-care plan and seek new strategies when necessary.
- **Benefits:** Ensures continued relevance and effectiveness of your mental health practices.

### 2. Seek Continuous Improvement:

- **What to Do:** Pursue personal growth and development throughout your life.
- **How to Do It:** Set new goals, seek feedback, and remain open to learning.
- **Benefits:** Supports ongoing fulfillment and adaptability.

### 3. Promote Mental Health Awareness:

- **What to Do:** Advocate for mental health awareness and support in your community.
- **How to Do It:** Participate in or organize awareness campaigns, share information, and support mental health initiatives.
- **Benefits:** Contributes to a more supportive and understanding society.

## Conclusion

Maintaining mental health over the long term involves a combination of ongoing support, self-care, and adaptation to life's changes. By staying informed, building supportive networks, and practicing personalized self-care, you can foster a fulfilling and resilient life. Addressing challenges proactively and embracing flexibility ensures that your approach to mental health remains effective and relevant. Ultimately, a commitment to continuous growth, reflection, and adaptation will support your mental well-being throughout life.

**How can I stay motivated?**

Staying motivated can be challenging, especially when juggling multiple responsibilities or facing obstacles. However, maintaining motivation is crucial for achieving personal and professional goals. Here are several strategies to help you stay motivated over the long term:

## 1. Set Clear and Meaningful Goals

**1. Define Your Goals:**

- **What to Do:** Set specific, measurable, achievable, relevant, and time-bound (SMART) goals.
- **How to Do It:** Break down larger goals into smaller, manageable tasks and set deadlines for each.
- **Benefits:** Provides clarity and a structured plan for what you want to achieve.

**2. Connect with Your Why:**

- **What to Do:** Understand and articulate why your goals are important to you.
- **How to Do It:** Reflect on the personal values or long-term benefits that your goals represent.
- **Benefits:** Increases intrinsic motivation by aligning your actions with your core values.

**3. Set Milestones and Celebrate Achievements:**

- **What to Do:** Establish milestones to track progress and celebrate when you reach them.
- **How to Do It:** Recognize and reward yourself for achieving both small and large milestones.
- **Benefits:** Provides a sense of accomplishment and keeps motivation high.

## 2. Create a Positive Environment

**1. Build a Support System:**

- **What to Do:** Surround yourself with supportive people who encourage and motivate you.
- **How to Do It:** Seek out mentors, join groups or communities related to your interests, and communicate with friends and family.
- **Benefits:** Offers encouragement and accountability, making it easier to stay motivated.

**2. Remove Distractions:**

- **What to Do:** Identify and minimize distractions in your environment.
- **How to Do It:** Create a dedicated workspace, use apps or tools to block distractions, and set boundaries for focused work periods.
- **Benefits:** Enhances focus and productivity, helping you stay on track with your goals.

**3. Organize Your Space:**

- **What to Do:** Maintain a clutter-free and organized workspace.
- **How to Do It:** Regularly clean and organize your environment to create a conducive work atmosphere.
- **Benefits:** Reduces stress and increases efficiency, which can boost motivation.

## 3. Develop and Maintain Productive Habits

**1. Create a Routine:**

- **What to Do:** Establish a daily or weekly routine that includes time for work, exercise, and relaxation.
- **How to Do It:** Plan your day with specific time blocks for different activities.
- **Benefits:** Builds consistency and makes it easier to stay motivated by creating a predictable structure.

**2. Use Time Management Techniques:**

- **What to Do:** Implement techniques like the Pomodoro Technique, time blocking, or task prioritization.
- **How to Do It:** Break tasks into smaller intervals and focus on one task at a time.
- **Benefits:** Enhances productivity and makes tasks feel more manageable, which can sustain motivation.

### 3. Focus on Progress, Not Perfection:

- **What to Do:** Emphasize the progress you're making rather than striving for perfection.
- **How to Do It:** Celebrate incremental progress and learn from setbacks.
- **Benefits:** Reduces pressure and keeps motivation high by acknowledging achievements.

## 4. Stay Inspired and Energized

### 1. Find Your Sources of Inspiration:

- **What to Do:** Identify what inspires and motivates you, such as books, podcasts, or people.
- **How to Do It:** Regularly engage with these sources to maintain enthusiasm and drive.
- **Benefits:** Keeps your motivation levels high by fueling your passion and interest.

### 2. Visualize Success:

- **What to Do:** Use visualization techniques to imagine achieving your goals.
- **How to Do It:** Spend a few minutes each day picturing your success and the positive outcomes associated with it.
- **Benefits:** Strengthens your commitment and reinforces your motivation.

### 3. Set Up a Reward System:

- **What to Do:** Create a reward system to celebrate milestones and achievements.
- **How to Do It:** Decide on small rewards for achieving tasks and larger rewards for reaching major goals.
- **Benefits:** Provides additional motivation and reinforces positive behavior.

## 5. Address Challenges and Obstacles

### 1. Develop Resilience:

- **What to Do:** Cultivate resilience by learning to cope with setbacks and maintain a positive outlook.
- **How to Do It:** Practice problem-solving, seek support when needed, and focus on solutions rather than problems.

- **Benefits:** Helps you bounce back from challenges and continue working towards your goals.

## 2. Reevaluate and Adjust Goals:

- **What to Do:** Regularly assess your goals and make adjustments as needed.
- **How to Do It:** Reflect on your progress and modify your goals based on changing circumstances or new insights.
- **Benefits:** Ensures that your goals remain relevant and achievable, keeping you motivated.

## 3. Manage Stress and Avoid Burnout:

- **What to Do:** Implement stress management techniques to maintain your well-being.
- **How to Do It:** Use relaxation techniques, take breaks, and maintain a healthy work-life balance.
- **Benefits:** Prevents burnout and maintains your motivation and energy levels.

# 6. Stay Accountable

## 1. Track Your Progress:

- **What to Do:** Keep a record of your progress towards your goals.
- **How to Do It:** Use journals, apps, or spreadsheets to monitor your achievements and setbacks.
- **Benefits:** Provides a sense of accomplishment and helps you stay focused on your objectives.

## 2. Share Your Goals with Others:

- **What to Do:** Communicate your goals and progress with a trusted friend, mentor, or accountability partner.
- **How to Do It:** Regularly update them on your progress and discuss any challenges you're facing.
- **Benefits:** Provides additional motivation and accountability.

## 3. Join Accountability Groups:

- **What to Do:** Participate in groups or communities that focus on goal-setting and accountability.

- **How to Do It:** Find or create groups where members share their goals and progress regularly.
- **Benefits:** Offers support and encouragement from others with similar objectives.

## Conclusion

Staying motivated involves setting clear and meaningful goals, creating a positive environment, developing productive habits, finding inspiration, addressing challenges, and maintaining accountability. By implementing these strategies, you can enhance your motivation and make steady progress towards your personal and professional goals. Remember, motivation can fluctuate, so it's important to regularly revisit and adjust your strategies to stay aligned with your evolving needs and aspirations.

**Bonus Chapter :**

- **Chapter 19: Mental Health Resources**
- **Hotlines,**
- **websites,**
- **additional reading recommendations**

Access to mental health resources is crucial for finding support, guidance, and information. Here is a comprehensive list of resources, including hotlines, websites, and reading recommendations, that can help you address mental health concerns:

## Hotlines

**1. National Suicide Prevention Lifeline**

- **Number:** 988 (U.S.)
- **Website:** 988 Lifeline
- **Description:** Provides 24/7, free, and confidential support for people in distress or crisis.

**2. Crisis Text Line**

- **Number:** Text HOME to 741741 (U.S. and Canada)
- **Website:** Crisis Text Line

- **Description:** Offers free, confidential support via text message for those in crisis.

## **3. Samaritans

- **Number:** 116 123 (UK and Ireland)
- **Website:** Samaritans
- **Description:** Provides 24/7 support for anyone in emotional distress or crisis.

## **4. Lifeline

- **Number:** 13 11 14 (Australia)
- **Website:** Lifeline
- **Description:** Offers crisis support and suicide prevention services 24/7.

## **5. National Domestic Violence Hotline

- **Number:** 1-800-799-SAFE (7233) (U.S.)
- **Website:** The Hotline
- **Description:** Provides support for individuals experiencing domestic violence.

## Websites

## **1. National Institute of Mental Health (NIMH)

- **Website:** NIMH
- **Description:** Offers comprehensive information on mental health disorders, research, and treatment options.

## **2. Mental Health America (MHA)

- **Website:** Mental Health America
- **Description:** Provides resources for mental health screenings, information, and advocacy.

## **3. Mind

- **Website:** Mind
- **Description:** Offers information and support for mental health issues, including resources for finding help.

## **4. The Trevor Project

- **Website:** The Trevor Project
- **Description:** Provides crisis intervention and suicide prevention services for LGBTQ+ youth.

****5. Headspace**

- **Website:** Headspace
- **Description:** Offers guided meditation and mindfulness exercises to support mental well-being.

****6. 7 Cups**

- **Website:** 7 Cups
- **Description:** Provides online emotional support through trained listeners and professional therapists.

## Additional Reading Recommendations

****1. "The Noonday Demon: An Atlas of Depression"** by Andrew Solomon

- **Description:** A comprehensive exploration of depression, including personal stories and scientific research.

****2. "Feeling Good: The New Mood Therapy"** by David D. Burns

- **Description:** Provides practical techniques based on cognitive-behavioral therapy (CBT) to combat depression.

****3. "The Body Keeps the Score: Brain, Mind, and Body in the Healing of Trauma"** by Bessel van der Kolk

- **Description:** Examines how trauma affects the body and mind and explores innovative therapies for healing.

****4. "Daring Greatly: How the Courage to Be Vulnerable Transforms the Way We Live, Love, Parent, and Lead"** by Brené Brown

- **Description:** Focuses on the power of vulnerability and its role in building meaningful connections and personal growth.

****5. "Lost Connections: Uncovering the Real Causes of Depression – and the Unexpected Solutions"** by Johann Hari

- **Description:** Explores the societal and personal factors contributing to depression and offers alternative solutions.

**6. "Radical Acceptance: Embracing Your Life With the Heart of a Buddha"** by Tara Brach

- **Description:** Combines mindfulness and self-compassion to help overcome feelings of unworthiness and embrace life fully.

**7. "The Happiness Trap: How to Stop Struggling and Start Living"** by Russ Harris

- **Description:** Provides insights from Acceptance and Commitment Therapy (ACT) to help readers improve their mental well-being.

## Conclusion

These resources offer a range of support options for mental health concerns. Whether you need immediate help, ongoing support, or additional information, utilizing these hotlines, websites, and reading materials can help you find the assistance and knowledge you need. Always remember that reaching out for support is a sign of strength, and there are many resources available to help you through challenging times.

What are some calming exercises?

Calming exercises can help reduce stress, manage anxiety, and promote relaxation. Here are some effective exercises to incorporate into your routine:

## 1. Deep Breathing

**1. Diaphragmatic Breathing:**

- **How to Do It:** Sit or lie down comfortably. Place one hand on your chest and the other on your abdomen. Inhale deeply through your nose, letting your abdomen rise more than your chest. Exhale slowly through your mouth.
- **Duration:** 5-10 minutes.
- **Benefits:** Activates the parasympathetic nervous system, helping to calm the mind and body.

**2. 4-7-8 Breathing:**

- **How to Do It:** Inhale quietly through your nose for 4 seconds, hold the breath for 7 seconds, and exhale completely through your mouth for 8 seconds.
- **Duration:** Repeat for 4-5 cycles.
- **Benefits:** Reduces anxiety and helps promote relaxation.

## 2. Progressive Muscle Relaxation (PMR)

### 1. Full-Body PMR:

- **How to Do It:** Sit or lie down comfortably. Start at your toes and work your way up to your head. Tense each muscle group (e.g., feet, calves, thighs, etc.) for 5-10 seconds, then relax for 20 seconds. Notice the contrast between tension and relaxation.
- **Duration:** 10-15 minutes.
- **Benefits:** Helps to identify and release physical tension and stress.

## 3. Mindfulness Meditation

### 1. Body Scan Meditation:

- **How to Do It:** Sit or lie down comfortably. Close your eyes and focus on each part of your body, starting from your toes and moving up to your head. Pay attention to any sensations, tension, or relaxation in each area.
- **Duration:** 10-20 minutes.
- **Benefits:** Increases body awareness and reduces stress by focusing on the present moment.

### 2. Guided Imagery:

- **How to Do It:** Find a quiet place and close your eyes. Visualize a peaceful scene, such as a beach or forest. Imagine the sights, sounds, and smells of this place, and immerse yourself in the experience.
- **Duration:** 5-15 minutes.
- **Benefits:** Creates a mental escape from stress and promotes relaxation.

## 4. Gentle Movement Exercises

**1. Yoga:**

- **How to Do It:** Practice gentle yoga poses such as Child's Pose, Cat-Cow, and Forward Fold. Focus on slow, deliberate movements and deep breathing.
- **Duration:** 15-30 minutes.
- **Benefits:** Combines physical movement with breath control to enhance relaxation.

**2. Tai Chi:**

- **How to Do It:** Perform slow, flowing movements with focused attention on breathing and posture.
- **Duration:** 20-30 minutes.
- **Benefits:** Promotes relaxation, balance, and mental clarity.

## 5. Grounding Techniques

**1. 5-4-3-2-1 Grounding:**

- **How to Do It:** Identify and name 5 things you can see, 4 things you can touch, 3 things you can hear, 2 things you can smell, and 1 thing you can taste.
- **Duration:** A few minutes.
- **Benefits:** Helps to anchor you in the present moment and reduce anxiety.

**2. Sensory Grounding:**

- **How to Do It:** Use sensory items (e.g., a soft blanket, calming essential oils, soothing music) to engage your senses and create a calming environment.
- **Duration:** Variable.
- **Benefits:** Engages the senses to promote relaxation and focus.

## 6. Journaling

**1. Gratitude Journaling:**

- **How to Do It:** Write down three things you're grateful for each day. Reflect on positive experiences and moments.
- **Duration:** 5-10 minutes daily.
- **Benefits:** Shifts focus to positive aspects of life and reduces stress.

## 2. Stream of Consciousness Writing:

- **How to Do It:** Write continuously for a set amount of time (e.g., 5-10 minutes) without worrying about grammar or structure. Let your thoughts flow freely.
- **Duration:** 5-10 minutes.
- **Benefits:** Helps to process emotions and reduce mental clutter.

# 7. Self-Massage

## 1. Hand Massage:

- **How to Do It:** Use your thumb and fingers to gently massage the palms, fingers, and wrists of one hand. Repeat with the other hand.
- **Duration:** 5 minutes per hand.
- **Benefits:** Reduces physical tension and promotes relaxation.

## 2. Neck and Shoulder Massage:

- **How to Do It:** Use your fingers to gently massage your neck and shoulders, applying light pressure and focusing on areas of tension.
- **Duration:** 5-10 minutes.
- **Benefits:** Alleviates muscle tension and promotes a sense of calm.

# 8. Breathing with Movement

## 1. Box Breathing:

- **How to Do It:** Inhale through your nose for 4 seconds, hold for 4 seconds, exhale through your mouth for 4 seconds, and pause for 4 seconds before repeating.
- **Duration:** 3-5 minutes.
- **Benefits:** Calms the nervous system and enhances focus.

## 2. Alternate Nostril Breathing:

- **How to Do It:** Use your right thumb to close your right nostril. Inhale deeply through your left nostril, then close it with your right ring finger. Exhale through your right nostril, and repeat.

- **Duration:** 5-10 minutes.
- **Benefits:** Balances the nervous system and promotes relaxation.

## Conclusion

Incorporating these calming exercises into your routine can help manage stress, enhance relaxation, and improve overall well-being. Experiment with different techniques to find what works best for you and integrate them into your daily or weekly schedule to maintain a sense of calm and balance.

- **Personal stories of people managing mental health for inspiration.**

Personal stories can be incredibly inspiring and provide valuable insights into managing mental health. Here are some real-life examples of people who have successfully navigated their mental health challenges and found ways to thrive:

### **1. Andrew Solomon

**Background:** Andrew Solomon is an acclaimed author and professor who has written extensively about depression and mental health. His book, *"The Noonday Demon: An Atlas of Depression,"* explores his own struggles with depression and the broader implications of mental illness.

**Story:** Solomon describes his battle with depression in candid detail, illustrating how it affected his personal and professional life. Despite the intense struggles, he sought help through therapy and medication, which significantly improved his condition. His journey underscores the importance of seeking professional help and finding a treatment plan that works for you.

**Inspiration:** Solomon's story highlights that mental health challenges are complex and personal but that with appropriate support and treatment, it is possible to manage symptoms and lead a fulfilling life. His work emphasizes the importance of understanding mental illness from both a personal and societal perspective.

## **2. J.K. Rowling

**Background:** J.K. Rowling, the famous author of the *Harry Potter* series, has spoken openly about her battle with depression and how it influenced her writing.

**Story:** Rowling struggled with severe depression in the early 1990s, during which she faced financial difficulties and a sense of overwhelming despair. Writing became a lifeline for her, providing both a creative outlet and a means to cope with her emotions. She has credited therapy and a supportive network of friends for helping her through this challenging period.

**Inspiration:** Rowling's experience demonstrates that creative pursuits and support systems can be powerful tools in managing mental health. Her story also illustrates that recovery is possible and that finding personal outlets for expression can play a critical role in healing.

## **3. Dwayne "The Rock" Johnson

**Background:** Dwayne Johnson, a well-known actor and former professional wrestler, has been open about his experiences with depression and mental health struggles.

**Story:** Johnson has shared that he faced depression during his early years as a professional wrestler and actor. He talked about how he initially struggled with the stigma around mental health and his reluctance to seek help. Eventually, he reached out for support and found solace in physical exercise, a strong support system, and openly discussing his experiences.

**Inspiration:** Johnson's story serves as a powerful reminder that even those in the public eye are not immune to mental health challenges. His openness about seeking help and using his platform to raise awareness demonstrates that mental health struggles are common and that speaking out and seeking support are essential steps toward recovery.

## **4. Brené Brown

**Background:** Brené Brown is a research professor and author known for her work on vulnerability, courage, and empathy. Her book, *"Daring Greatly,"* addresses the importance of embracing vulnerability in managing mental health.

**Story:** Brown's research and personal experiences have highlighted how embracing vulnerability and practicing self-compassion can profoundly impact mental health. She has shared her own journey of dealing with shame and insecurity, emphasizing that acknowledging and accepting these feelings is crucial for emotional well-being.

**Inspiration:** Brown's insights into vulnerability and shame offer valuable lessons on self-acceptance and resilience. Her approach encourages people to embrace their authentic selves and seek support when needed, which can significantly enhance mental health.

## **5. Chrissy Teigen

**Background:** Chrissy Teigen, a model and television personality, has been open about her struggles with postpartum depression and anxiety.

**Story:** Teigen publicly shared her experiences with postpartum depression after the birth of her first child. She spoke about the challenges she faced and how it affected her daily life. By sharing her story, she not only sought support but also helped break the stigma surrounding postpartum depression, encouraging others to seek help and talk openly about their struggles.

**Inspiration:** Teigen's story highlights the importance of addressing postpartum mental health issues and the power of speaking out to reduce stigma. Her openness and advocacy work encourage others to seek support and understand that they are not alone in their experiences.

## **6. Jesse Jackson

**Background:** Jesse Jackson is a civil rights leader and politician who has spoken publicly about his battle with Parkinson's disease and depression.

**Story:** Jackson has been open about his struggles with Parkinson's disease and how it has affected his mental health. He has used his platform to discuss the challenges of living with a chronic illness and the importance of mental health care in managing such conditions. His advocacy emphasizes the interconnectedness of physical and mental health.

**Inspiration:** Jackson's story underscores the importance of addressing both physical and mental health issues together. His openness about his experiences with Parkinson's disease and depression encourages others to seek comprehensive care and support.

## **7. Selena Gomez

**Background:** Selena Gomez is a singer and actress who has been candid about her struggles with anxiety and depression, as well as her diagnosis with lupus.

**Story:** Gomez has openly discussed her mental health challenges, including her experiences with anxiety and depression, as well as her lupus diagnosis. She has shared how therapy, medication, and self-care practices have helped her manage her mental health. Gomez also uses her platform to advocate for mental health awareness and support.

**Inspiration:** Gomez's story highlights the importance of self-care, therapy, and medication in managing mental health. Her advocacy work helps to normalize mental health struggles and encourage others to seek help.

## Conclusion

These personal stories offer inspiration and insight into managing mental health challenges. They highlight the importance of seeking help, finding supportive outlets, and openly discussing mental health issues. By sharing their experiences, these individuals provide hope and encouragement for others facing similar struggles, emphasizing that recovery and management are possible with the right support and strategies.

**"May you enjoy good health and happiness now and always."**

Lucien Gahiel